BO

karate weapon of self~defense

BO
karate weapon of self~defense

by Fumio Demura

© 1976 Ohara Publications, Incorporated
All rights reserved
Printed in the United States of America
Library of Congress Catalog Card Number 76-13757

Thirty-second printing 1999

ISBN-0-89750-019-9

Graphic Design by Nancy Hom Lem
Photography by Ed Ikuta

WARNING

OHARA  PUBLICATIONS, INCORPORATED

SANTA CLARITA, CALIFORNIA

dedication

To the late Okinawan karate master, Kenshin Taira, that perfect example of the gentle spirit of the martial arts, who was initially responsible for my interest and subsequent skill in kobu-do; and to Yasutsune Itosu and Kenwa Mabuni, revered masters who are the grandfathers of modern kobu-do and karate.

acknowledgements

I would like to express my thanks to Chuck Lanza, Gladys Caldwell and Larry Carlson for their help with the preparation of this book; and to Makoto Ibushi and Paul Godshaw for their assistance as my partners in the photographs.

about the author

Fumio Demura, 5th-dan, was born in Yokohama, Japan. He began his martial arts training during his grammar school years, studying kendo to build up his strength and improve his health. When his instructor moved out of the area, Mr. Demura transferred to a dojo that taught both karate and kendo. In high school, he also studied aikido and later, judo. While at Nihon University in Tokyo, he earned a Bachelor of Science degree in economics. Concurrently, he developed a keen interest in all martial arts, including the use of weapons such as the *bo*, the *sai*, the *tonfa*, the *kama* and the *nunchaku*. These weaponry techniques he studied while under the tutelage of Mr. Kenshin Taira and Mr. Ryusho Sakagami.

Noted in Japan as an outstanding karateka, Mr. Demura has been honored by martial artists and government officials alike. In 1961, he won the All-Japan Karate Free-Style Tournament and, for three consecutive years (from 1961 to 1964), was lauded as one of Japan's top eight players. His numerous tournament wins include the East Japan, the Shito-Ryu Annual and the Kanto District championships. Mr. Demura also received the All-Japan Karate Federation President's trophy for outstanding tournament play and, for his outstanding achievements in and contributions to the art of karate, he was awarded certificates of recognition by such Japanese Cabinet officials as the Ministers of Education, Finance and Transportation.

In response to an invitation from Mr. Dan Ivan, Mr. Demura came to the United States in 1965 to teach Shito-Ryu, one of the world's four major systems of karate. He now heads his own dojo in Santa Ana, California, and supervises classes at the Irvine campus of the University of California, Orange Coast College and Riverside City College. He also directs the U.S. division of the Japan Karate Federation and serves as an advisor for the Pan-American Karate Association.

In addition, Mr. Demura endures a strenuous round of demonstrations and exhibitions. While there, his presentations were a large part of the attraction enjoyed by the now defunct Japanese Village in Buena Park, California. His current schedule includes karate and samurai shows at the Las Vegas Hilton in Las Vegas, Nevada, and Marineland in Redondo Beach, California. In 1973, he also found time to co-star in a Hong Kong-based cinema production.

In 1969, BLACK BELT Magazine's Hall of Fame paid tribute to the author's dedication to karate by presenting him with its much coveted Karate Sensei of the Year Award. In 1974, he received the martial arts' Golden Fist award and, in 1975, was further honored by the BLACK BELT Hall of Fame's designation, Martial Artist of the Year.

Mr. Demura's first book, *Shito-Ryu Karate*, was published in 1971. His second and third works, *Nunchaku, Karate Weapon of Self-Defense* and *Sai, Karate Weapon of Self-Defense*, both deal with kobu-do and were published in 1971 and 1974, respectively.

contents

history of the bo (or kon)

As with many weapons of ancient heritage, the exact origin of the *bo*, *kon* or straight staff is obscure. Anthropologists know, however, that it was among the first tools used by early man to help him survive. Initially, it took the form of a stick, a branch from a tree or a club and was used both to defend against attackers and to help acquire food. Over the ages, the use of the bo or kon as a weapon has been developed and refined. Still, because modern practitioners hesitate over the exact details of its evolution, several theories on the history of the bo, as it is known today, prevail.

Whether factual or not, one very popular theory (related to the author by his masters) provides the following rendition of this history: Around 517 A.D., the Zen Buddhist priest Daruma Daishi, the leader of the Shorin-ji Temple in China, brought into effect fluent use of the bo. During this period of Chinese history, government control was minimal and law and order belonged only to those capable of securing it for themselves. For Daruma and his disciples, proficiency in the martial arts and the use of weapons such as the spear, the *sai* (a short sword with two prongs at the handle), and the bo provided the only feasible means of protecting their temple. The bo-jitsu techniques Daruma ordered his disciples to master and perfect greatly influenced the later development of *Ryukyu Kobu-Do*.

Ryukyu Kobu-Do, the Okinawan art of using karate weapons

such as the bo, the sai, the *kama* (sickle) and the *nunchaku* (two hardwood sticks connected by rope or chain), first gained prominence around 1314 A.D. when the Japanese government passed two laws which deeply outraged the people of Okinawa. First, it barred all inhabitants of the island from owning or possessing any sort of lethal weapon. Second, it imposed on them a monumental increase in taxes. Deprived of any conventional means of physical protest or retaliation, the people turned not only to empty-handed martial arts forms for protection, but to their farm implements as well, using them as weapons which eventually became the *tonfa*, the nunchaku, the kama, the *kai* (boat oar) and the bo. The bo itself originated with the *tenbin*, a stick held across the shoulders, usually with buckets hanging from each end, that was used to convey food, water or some such. When the need arose, the tenbin, or the bo as it is known today, was manipulated to strike or block in techniques either based on or very similar to those used by Daruma and his disciples.

masters of kobu~do

More than karate or any other popular martial art, sources of information on kobu-do are scarce. Kobu-do dojo able to teach students anything of value, are rare. Many styles, kata (exercises or forms) and techniques have accompanied their creators into eternal oblivion because records of the art's development are virtually non-existent. Compounding this lack of kobu-do material, much of the art was practiced and developed in utter secrecy—in the nighttime darkness of covert mountain retreats or sealed off in similar places, safe from penetration by intruding eyes.

To help alleviate this famine of kobu-do information, the few masters of *bo-jitsu* (the art of using the bo) known to this author are presented here.

Shinken Taira

Shinken Taira was born in 1890 (the 33rd year of Meiji) in Kumijima City on the island of Okinawa. In 1923, he began studying karate under Master Gichin Funakoshi, founder of the art, and later, received intensive Okinawan kobu-do instruction from Master Mouden Yahishisa. After many years of rigorous training, he earned his Master's Degree and moved to Ikaho City in Gunma prefecture, Japan. There he opened the first of many dojo and taught both karate and kobu-do. In 1940 (the 15th year of Showa), he returned to Okinawa and, in Naha, established a dojo devoted to the art of kobu-do. Although Master Taira passed away in 1970, the art lives on and flourishes through his students. One of them, Fumio Demura, has become a leading exponent of kobu-do.

Sueyoshi

While it is known that Master Sueyoshi was born sometime during the early 1900s, with one exception no other details of his life have been recorded. This one exception is his kata for the bo, *Sueyoshi-No-Kon*.

Toyama

Born in the early 1900s, Master Toyama founded the style of bo-jitsu called *Toyama-Ryu-Bo-Jitsu* and his kata, *Toyama-No-Kon*, remains for modern students to practice.

Chinen of Yamane-Ryu

Born in the early 1900s, Master Chinen's extensive studies of bo-jitsu made him a specialist in the art. He developed many kata for the bo, among them *Shushi-No-Kon*, *Shirotaru-No-Kon* (known in Okinawa as *Ogusuku*) and *Yonegawa-No-Kon* (*Gyaku-Bo*). Several of his students later became famous karateka renowned for their proficiency in kobu-do.

Aragaki

Master Aragaki, also born in the early 1900s, founded the *Aragaki-Ryu* style of kobu-do. His particular specialties were bo-jitsu and sai-jitsu (the art of using the sai).

Tsuken

Master Tsuken, born in the late 1800s, formulated a kata called *Tsuken-Hantagawa-No-Kon* (also known as *Tsuken-Bo*) which was the culmination of all his kobu-do training. It was characterized by a certain twist known as *gyaku-bo* or reverse or left-handed bo.

Miyazato

Apart from dating his birth sometime during the late 1800s, the only records available on Master Miyazato tell of his pilgrimage to China. There he studied not only "empty-handed" martial arts but the use of weapons as well. Eventually enjoying great renown as a martial artist, Master Miyazato was reputedly invincible in the art of bo-jitsu. The movements of his kata, *Miyazato-Bo*, seem to reflect his strength and vigor.

Sueishi

Born sometime during the mid-1800s, Master Sueishi belonged to a very prominent samurai family living in Shuri on the island of Okinawa. Although he received instruction in many different styles of kobu-do, his specialty was bo-jitsu. He formulated two very precise and beautiful bo-jitsu kata known as *Sueishi-No-Kon* and *Shoun-No-Kon.*

Shitanaka Chinen

Born into a poor family of the late 1800s, Master Chinen originally came to Master Sueishi only to serve as his houseboy. Yet, for many months, he would secretly watch his master's martial arts classes, absorbing as much of it as he could. Then, between chores, he would go off alone and practice different techniques. Eventually, Master Sueishi became aware of the boy's interest. Watching the youth practice and impressed with the deep and passionate feelings Chinen had for the martial arts, he granted the boy permission to attend formal lessons. Master Chinen studied both bo-jitsu and sai-jitsu and later developed *Chinen-Shitanaka-No-Kon*, a beautiful kata with very precise, polished movements.

Sakugawa

Master Sakugawa was born during the mid-1800s in Suri on the island of Akata, Okinawa. As with Master Miyazato, his thirst for more expertise in kobu-do led him to China. There he studied the use of the bo and other traditional Chinese weapons. On returning to Okinawa, he devised many dynamic, powerful kata, the most famous of which is *Sakugawa-No-Kon.*

Donchi Ginowan

A foremost pupil of Master Sakugawa, Master Ginowan's own skill in kobu-do was formidable and, after Master Sakugawa's death, reputedly unsurpassed. However, the dynamism and power which marked his bo-jitsu and sai-jitsu styles were such that they bordered on imitations of his late sensei's methods.

Tsuken Kouruguwa

Very little background information exists on Master Kouruguwa apart from the fact that, as a very accomplished master of kobu-do, he developed the bo-jitsu kata *Urazoe-No-Bo-Kon* and the Kouruguwa style of using the sai.

Nakanhari No Jii

Unfortunately, outside of his reputation as an overwhelming kobu-do artist, no information on Master Nakanhari exists. Even his particular style is unknown.

Matsumura

An expert in both karate and the use of weapons, Master Matsumura's "empty-handed" training heavily influenced his style of kobu-do which became known as *Matsumura-Ryu.*

Akahachi Oyakei

Born in the mid-1700s on the island of Yaeyama, Okinawa, stories and legends indicate that Master Oyakei was the strongest, most accomplished bo-jitsu man of his time. His bo-jitsu legacy to contemporary students is the kata *Akahachi-No-Gyakubo* (reverse or left-handed bo).

kobu~do bo~jitsu kata

Bo-jitsu kata are exercises or forms consisting of a set sequence of bo techniques and movements. As with information on the origin, past masters and history of kobu-do, many of these kata have been lost or forgotten. Those that still exist have been handed down through the years from master to pupil and bear the names of the experts who devised them:

Shushi-No-Kon-Dai	Shitanaka-No-Kon
Shushi-No-Kon-Sho	Sueyoshi-No-Kon
Sakugawa-No-Kon-Dai	Soeishi-No-Kon
Sakugawa-No-Kon-Sho	Aragaki-No-Kon
Shoun-No-Kon	Tenryu-No-Kon
Hakuson-No-Kon	Sunakake-No-Kon
Yonegawa-No-Kon	Tsuken-Bo
Chinen-Shitahaku-No-Kon	Teruya-No-Kon
Suezoko-No-Kon	Oshiro-No-Kon
Urazoe-No-Kon	Chibana-No-Kon

kinds and types of bo

Although the actual size and dimensions of a bo depend on the individual student's needs, the standard bo or kon is the straight, six-foot-long *roku shaku-bo*. Measuring 1¼-inch thick at its center, it tapers out to a ¾-inch thickness at each end. This tapered structure functions in several ways: (1) It insures an even balance and guarantees that the bo's fulcrum stays at its center. (2) It facilitates easy handling and effortless maneuvering. (3) It reduces rigidity and increases the bo's tensile strength, thereby diminishing breakage and (4) making possible strong, powerful whipping, striking and blocking actions.

While most bo possess this tapered structure, they do vary in length and shape. Apart from the standard six-foot measurement, bo range anywhere from four feet in length (*yon shaku-bo*) to nine feet in length (*kyu-shaku-bo*). They are usually round or circular at the center and maintain this shape as they taper out. Although modern students use the circularly-shaped bo almost exclusively, early practitioners of bo-jitsu often took square, hexagonal or octagonal shaped bo into combat because the multiple edges provided a more destructive effect.

Contemporary bo-jitsu men use strong, hard wood, preferably red or white oak, in the construction of their weapons. In earlier days, however, strong bamboo was sometimes substituted for the wood, resulting in a surprisingly sturdy and effective bo.

KINDS AND TYPES OF BO

A. **Maru-Bo** (Round)

B. **Kaku-Bo** (Four-Sided)

C. **Rokkaku-Bo** (Six-Sided)

D. **Hakkaku-Bo** (Eight-Sided)

E. **Take-Bo** (Bamboo)

F. **Yari** (Spear)

G. **Naginata** (Long Sword)

H. **Kai** (Oar)

Sketch A shows the most common circularly-shaped type of bo. Sketches B through E show the types of bo often used by early practitioners of bo-jitsu. While the weapons shown in sketches F through G are not technically part of the bo family, in practice, regular bo-jitsu techniques are used to handle and maneuver them. As such, they may be classified as different types of bo.

ANATOMY OF THE STANDARD BO

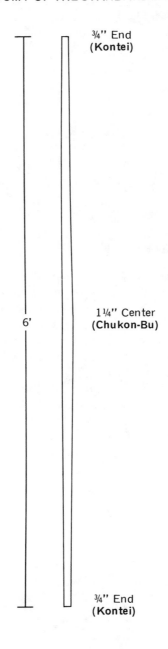

¾" End
(Kontei)

6'

1¼" Center
(Chukon-Bu)

¾" End
(Kontei)

storage of the bo

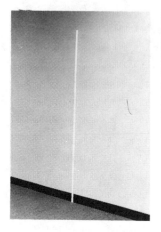

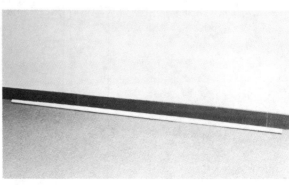

Proper Storage Positions

Proper storage of the bo when it is not in use entails either standing it vertically and completely upright or laying it down horizontally. In either case, the bo must be supported by backing along its entire length. It should never be propped up at an angle nor should it hang on the wall horizontally resting on two hooks (or nails). These methods of storage cause warping and destroy the weapon's natural maneuverability.

A good test for determining whether a bo possesses its proper shape and handling qualities (either initially or after a long storage period) is to roll it across a flat surface. If structurally sound, it will roll smoothly and with little noise. If warped or bent, it will roll unevenly, making a loud clatter with each revolution.

Testing the Bo

holding the bo

THE BASIC GRIP

Whether they involve a single movement or a series of complex combinations, almost all bo-jitsu executions demand clutching the bo with the basic grip.

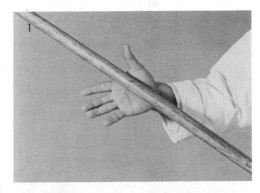

(1) To grasp the bo properly, place it across your open palm. (2) Then, beginning with your little finger, wrap all four digits around the shaft. (3) Fold your thumb over your forefinger as you would in a karate fist.

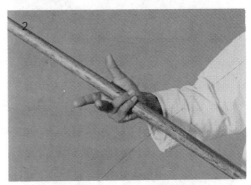

Sideview of (3)

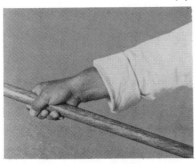

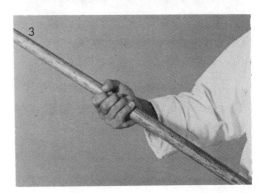

BASIC HOLDS

Execution of bo-jitsu techniques requires familiarity with four basic holding positions: *jun nigiri* (basic hold), *gyaku nigiri* (reverse hold), *yose nigiri* (double hold) and *hasami nigiri* (palm hold).

JUN NIGIRI (Basic Hold)
Using both hands in the basic grip, place them about a shoulder-width apart and centered along the length of the weapon. Hold the bo across your body at a 45-degree angle, the palm of your upper hand facing the ceiling, the palm of your lower hand facing the floor. The jun nigiri is used primarily for striking and other offensive movements.

GYAKU NIGIRI (Reverse Hold)
Using both hands in the basic grip, place them about a shoulder-width apart and centered along the length of the weapon. Hold the bo across your body horizontally, both palms facing the floor. While primarily a defensive position used to block or keep out of an opponent's range, the gyaku nigiri may sometimes double as an offensive hold.

YOSE NIGIRI (Double Hold)

Using both hands in the basic grip, place them next to each other toward one end of the bo. Hold the staff as you would a baseball bat: at an angle, the palm of your upper hand toward the ceiling, the palm of your lower hand toward the floor. This position functions both offensively and defensively and may be used against multiple opponents in a wide, swinging arc.

HASAMI NIGIRI (Palm Hold)

Hold the bo vertically before you, one hand even with your forehead, the other at waist level, both centered along the length of the weapon. Do not use the basic grip but, keeping both hands open, grasp the shaft securely with only your thumbs, forefingers and palms. Both palms should face the ceiling. Basically a defensive position, the hasami nigiri allows smooth, easy movement in almost any direction.

FEELING AND AWARENESS EXERCISE

The feeling and awareness exercise helps develop kinesthetic familiarity with holding and maneuvering the bo. At first, perform the exercise slowly and smoothly. Then, as you become more proficient, increase your speed of execution but continue to maintain a smoothness in your movements back and forth. This smoothness insures maximum results.

(1) Holding the bo across your body in a horizontal hasami nigiri (as opposed to the vertical one shown earlier), place your right hand—palm toward the ceiling—at the bo's center, your left hand—palm toward the floor—over toward the staff's left end. (2) With your right hand acting as a fulcrum, begin rotating the bo in a counterclockwise movement before you. Simultaneously, slide your left hand up the shaft. (3) As the bo reaches a vertical position, forming a 90-degree angle with the floor, your

hands should be parallel to it and to each other, your left hand situated slightly below your right. (4) Continue the counterclockwise rotation. However, now use your left hand as the fulcrum and slide your right hand down past it toward what is becoming the right end of the staff. (5) Then, when the bo again reaches a horizontal position, your left hand —palm toward the ceiling—should be at the bo's center, your right hand— palm toward the floor—over toward the right end of the staff.

warming~up exercises

The warming-up calisthenics presented here should be performed prior to every training or practice session. They help improve your overall dexterity with the bo and insure that you maintain proper finger control, wrist action, weight shiftings and shoulder and hip twisting.

BALANCE AND COORDINATION EXERCISE
(1) Hold the bo across your body horizontally, placing your open right hand—palm toward the ceiling—under the bo's center, your open left hand—palm toward the floor—over toward the left end of the weapon (as at the start of the feeling and awareness exercise). (2) Using both arms, begin rotating the bo in a counterclockwise movement. (3) Simultaneously, slide your left hand up the shaft and your right hand down to it so that (4) as the bo completes a 180-degree counterclockwise rotation and is again parallel to the floor, your open left hand—palm toward

the ceiling—supports its center and your open right hand—palm toward the floor—touches a spot near what is now its right end. (5) Now, use both arms to begin a clockwise rotation of the bo. (6) Simultaneously, slide your right hand up the shaft and your left hand down it so that (7) as the bo completes a 180-degree clockwise rotation, your hands return to their original positions: open right hand—palm toward the ceiling—under the staff's center, open left hand—palm toward the floor—at a spot near its left end.

FINGER AND TWIRLING EXERCISE

(1) Using only the fore- and middle-fingers of your right hand, grasp the bo near its center. Curl your forefinger around the top of the staff and secure it from beneath with the back of your middle finger. Turn your palm toward you and hold the weapon horizontally before you at head level. (2) Gently pushing down and away on it with your left hand, begin a twirling, counterclockwise rotation of the bo. Use your right hand as a fulcrum and turn your wrist counterclockwise to accommodate the rotation. (3) As the bo revolves, turn your palm away from you. Simultaneously, manipulate your fingers, pushing with your thumb, (4) to complete a 360-degree counterclockwise revolution. Secure the bo between your forefinger, now resting underneath the weapon, and your middle finger, now positioned above it. (5) Curl your fingers over the bo, (6) slide your forefinger up and over also and, using the basic grip, take hold of the shaft. Continue the counterclockwise revolution for approximately 90 degrees. (7-8) Slip your forefinger back under the bo and, securing the weapon between the back of your forefinger and your middle finger, turn your wrist in the opposite direction to begin a clockwise twirl. (9) As the bo travels, turn your palm toward you. At the same time, manipulate your fingers and push with your thumb to complete a 360-degree clockwise revolution. As before, secure the weapon between your forefinger and the back of your middle finger. (10-11) To end the exercise, move your wrist and manipulate your fingers to execute a second counterclockwise twirl. (12) As the weapon completes a 360-degree turn, slide your forefinger over it and, palm facing away, use the basic grip to take hold of the bo.

"FIGURE EIGHT" EXERCISE

(1) With your right hand, palm toward the ceiling, grasp the bo near its center. Use the basic grip. Extend your arm comfortably before you at shoulder level and hold the bo in a horizontal position. (2) Trace a "figure eight" with the weapon: Smoothly turn the bo counterclockwise, using your hand as a fulcrum. As it completes a 180-degree rotation, your palm now toward the floor, begin moving the bo down and across toward your left hip. Rotate the staff counterclockwise at an additional 45 degrees so that it slides downward and across at an angle. (3) With the bo over on your left side, sweep it upward smoothly to shoulder level. At the same time, rotate it clockwise so that (4) at the height of the movement, your palm turns toward the ceiling. (5) Now, move the bo down and across toward your right hip. Increase the clockwise rotation so that

the staff slides downward and across at an angle. (6) With the bo over on your right side, sweep it upward smoothly to shoulder level. At the same time, rotate it counterclockwise so that (7) at the height of the movement, your palm faces the floor.

Coordinate the bo's rotations and movements down and across with a concurrent rotation of your shoulders and hips. This action insures a smooth, well-formed "figure eight." In addition, try to maintain the original angle of your elbow—that is, do not bend or straighten it to accommodate the bo's pattern of movement. Instead, let your shoulders and wrists do the maneuvering.

This exercise helps loosen and develop the muscles of the wrists, shoulders and torso. It also functions in sparring as both a defensive and offensive technique.

SHOULDER EXERCISE
(1) Using both hands in the basic grip, palms facing forward, hold the bo horizontally behind your back. Spread your hands about two shoulder-widths apart and centered along the length of the weapon. Keep your arms as straight as possible. (2) Without bending your elbows, raise the bo up behind you, (3) over your head and bring it down in front

slightly to a level even with your forehead. Your palms should now face backward. (4) Release your grip, letting the bo fall before you. Simultaneously, drop both your hands, open and palms toward the ceiling, to positions directly beneath it, (5) catching the staff at waist level.

This exercise encourages beneficial loosening of the shoulder muscles and improves hand/eye coordination.

HIP EXERCISE

(1-2) Using both hands in the basic grip, palms forward, hold the bo horizontally behind your back (as in the shoulder exercise). Twist your torso counterclockwise (that is, to the left) as far as possible. (3-4) Then, reverse

the movement and twist clockwise (that is, to the right) as far as possible. Alternately repeat twisting to the left and to the right.

For best results, keep your back and arms straight throughout the exercise.

STRIKING EXERCISE (Soburi)

(1) Using the yose nigiri (double hold), right hand uppermost, grasp one end of the bo. Do not place your hands next to each other, however, but space them approximately one forearm-length apart. Position the lower end of the staff near your abdomen. Extend your right arm directly before you so that the weapon forms a 45-degree angle with your body. (2) Pulling with your right hand, swing the upper end of the bo down to your right and angle it toward the floor. (3) Smoothly raise the staff to a horizontal position high above your head. (4) Then, strike

forward and down with it, returning to your original position. (5) Now, by crossing your right arm over your left, swing the upper end of the bo down to your left and angle it toward the floor. (6) Again, smoothly raise the staff high above your head. (7) Then, strike forward and down with it to return to your original position.

At the point of impact, your *kime* (focus of energy) must be at its fullest so you must concentrate intensely when striking. In addition, remember to maintain strict eye contact throughout.

THRUSTING EXERCISE

Performance of this exercise requires the assistance of a partner. As he stands approximately four to six paces in front of you, have him form a circle with the thumb and forefinger of one hand and hold it out to the side on a level even with his eyes.

(1) To assume the starting position, grasp the bo with the jun nigiri (basic hold), right hand uppermost. Slide your left hand down to hold the lower end of the staff securely. Place your right hand two shoulder-widths away from your left and loosen its grasp enough to give the staff free movement through it. Angling the bo along the left side of your body, aim its upper end toward the circle formed by your partner's fingers. (2) Keep your right arm stationary throughout the exercise. With a smooth, steady movement of your left hand, thrust the bo forward and (3) through your partner's circle. Continue thrusting until your left hand meets your right. (4) Pull the bo back to its starting position and repeat the exercise.

This exercise develops the coordination necessary for smooth, accurate thrusts. It should be repeated until proficient action is achieved.

stances

Effective execution of any martial art technique requires mastering stances which allow the greatest stability yet provide the most fluid movement. In kobu-do, these stances, identical to those found in karate, utilize a "total body" concept. As such, pay particular attention to maintaining sound balance, good posture and natural movement.

HEISOKU-DACHI (Ready Stance)
Stand erect, feet together. Hold your arms along your sides. Use this position prior to bowing.

MUSUBI-DACHI (Ready Stance)
Stand erect, heels together. Point your toes outward 45 degrees. Keep your arms along your sides. Hold the bo comfortably in your right hand, knuckles to the outside, and position it vertically behind your right arm and shoulder.

HEIKO-DACHI (Natural Stance)

Stand erect and position your feet approximately one shoulder-width apart, parallel to each other and pointing forward. Keep your arms along your sides. With your right hand, knuckles to the outside, hold the bo vertically in front of your right arm and shoulder in readiness for the next move.

SOTO-HACHIJI-DACHI (Natural Stance)

Stand erect and position your feet approximately one shoulder-width apart, toes pointed outward 45 degrees. Keep your arms along your sides and hold the bo vertically in front of your right arm and shoulder as in the heiko-dachi. The soto-hachiji-dachi is very similar to the *uchi-hachiji-dachi*. To assume the uchi-hachiji-dachi, which is not shown here, again position your feet approximately one shoulder-width apart. However, point your toes inward slightly, not outward.

ZENKUTSU-DACHI (Forward Stance)

Bend your forward leg at the knee and shift 60 percent of your weight to it. This helps propel a strong, forward momentum during blocking and attacking. Lock the knee of your rear leg and extend it approximately two shoulder-widths behind your lead foot. Do not lean forward but keep your torso erect.

SANCHIN-DACHI (Tension Stance)

Begin in the heiko-dachi. Keep your weight distributed evenly over both legs. Tense your knees and pull them inward. Slide your forward foot slightly ahead of your rear foot. Point the toes of both feet inward. Keep your back straight and your hips tensed. Use the sanchin-dachi for close in-fighting and blocking or for dynamic tension in breathing exercises.

NAIFANCHI-DACHI or
KIBA-DACHI (Horse Stance)

Spread your feet approximately two shoulder-widths apart, parallel to each other, toes pointed forward. Distribute your weight evenly over both legs and bend your knees, as in the shiko-daichi stance. Tighten all the muscles of your legs and hips. Remember to keep your back straight, your torso erect, and to push your chest out.

GYAKU-ZENKUTSU-DACHI
(Rear Defense Stance)

Position your feet, bend one knee and distribute your weight as you would in the zenkutsu-dachi. In this case, however, lead with your extended leg toward the opponent. Lean away from him over your bent knee. Turn your head and torso back toward your extended leg to face your adversary. Use this stance exclusively in defensive techniques such as retreats from rear attacks.

NEKOASHI-DACHI (Cat Stance)

Shift 90 percent of your weight to your rear leg. Bend your rear knee, keep your rear foot flat on the floor and turn both 90 degrees to the outside. Resting it lightly on the ball of your foot, put your right leg down before you about one shoulder-width away from your left. Crouch slightly as you bend your right knee also. Used primarily for defense, the nekoashi-dachi emphasizes mobility. It also allows combining kicks with your forward leg and strikes with the bo.

KOKUTSU-DACHI (Back Stance)

Shift at least 70 percent of your weight to your rear leg, bend your rear knee and turn both 90 degrees to the outside. Place your forward foot two shoulder-widths in front of and perpendicular to your rear foot. Used primarily to defend against frontal attacks, this stance not only allows free movement of your forward leg but also facilitates quick changes in position—simply shift your weight forward and assume a zenkutsu-dachi or some similar stance.

SHIKO-DACHI (Straddle Stance)
Spread your feet approximately two shoulder-widths apart, toes pointed outward at 45 degree angles. Distribute your weight evenly over both legs. Bend both knees deeply, pull them back as far as possible and keep your torso erect. This stance doubles as both a strong offensive and defensive position and provides a solid base for quick maneuvering to either side.

SHIRASAGIASHI-DACHI (Crane or One-Legged Stance)
Use this stance to defend yourself from a foot sweep or a weaponry attack to your legs. Raise the besieged foot and tuck it behind the knee of your other leg. Bend your supporting leg at the knee and turn its foot outward. At the same time, shift your body back out of range.

kamae or basic fighting positions

There are three kobu-do *kamae* or basic fighting positions—the forward fighting position, the rear fighting position and the kneeling position. Identical to the corresponding *no-kamae* or fighting stances of karate, all three lend themselves to the instinctive, fluidly mobile and well-balanced actions necessary for successful bo-jitsu performances.

The mobility allowed by the kobu-do kamae positions also facilitates countering and attacking from almost any angle. During training, practice using all three positions with both the *hidari-no-kamae* and the *migi-no-kamae* commands. These instruct assuming a position to cover either the left or the right flank, respectively. For instance, when given the hidari-no-kamae command for the forward fighting position, assume a right stance with your left leg protected in the rear. When given the migi-no-kamae command, assume a left stance with your right leg protected in the rear. Vigorous training using both commands and all three fighting positions helps insure proper movement to all directions.

THE FORWARD FIGHTING POSITION

Assume a left zenkutsu-dachi (forward stance). Hold the bo with the gyaku nigiri (reverse hold) and angle it on the right side of your body, your left hand uppermost and leading. In this case, following the migi-nokamae command, the position protects your rear right leg. To follow the hidari-no-kamae command, assume a right zenkutsu-dachi. The forward fighting position works best when used with striking techniques and it facilitates a wide variety of aggressive executions. In early times, the bo-jitsu fighter would assume this position and, swiftly sweeping the lower end of his weapon along the ground and up, shoot dirt into his opponent's eyes. With his adversary blinded, he would then finish him off with a thrust of the upper section of his staff.

THE REAR FIGHTING POSITION

Assume a left gyaku-zenkutsu-dachi (rear defense stance). Hold the bo near one end with the yose nigiri (double hold) but space your hands about one shoulder-width apart. Position the staff vertically near your right shoulder. In this instance, following the migi-no-kamae command, the position protects your rear right flank. Although the rear fighting position may be used in either offensive or defensive techniques, it functions most effectively when combined with striking maneuvers.

THE KNEELING POSITION

Kneel down on your right leg and prop yourself up on your left foot. Do not crouch but keep your torso erect. Using the hasami nigiri (palm hold), left hand uppermost, hold the bo next to your left leg and in front of your right knee. In this case, following the migi-no-kamai command, the position protects your rear right flank. The kneeling position is primarily a defensive movement used to counter low attacks and the like.

the yoi (ready) position

The *yoi* or ready position is usually assumed at the beginning and at the end of bo-jitsu kata (predetermined sequences of movements and techniques). It facilitates both a relaxed entry into and an easy exit out of the kata's actual applications.

After bowing, (1) assume a musubi-dachi (natural stance). With your right hand, thumb innermost, palm facing back, grasp the bo a little below its center. Hold it vertically behind your right arm and shoulder. Let your left arm hang naturally along your left side. (2-3) Using your right shoulder as a fulcrum, swing the bo across your body and angle it up toward the high left. (4) Pull your right hand inward, palm toward you at head level, and angle the staff toward the high right. Simultaneously, grasp it farther down the shaft in a left hasami nigiri (palm hold), palm toward the floor. (5) Then, pull down and forward with your right hand, palm toward the ceiling, and extend your right arm before you at shoulder level. Push up and to the right with your left hand, angling what is now the right end of the weapon toward the floor. Both palms should face the ceiling. (6) To enter the yoi (ready) position, keep your right elbow straight and bring the bo down vertically in front of your right arm and shoulder. Hold your left arm, bent at the elbow, horizontally across your face. (7) Move out of the yoi position by raising your left hand to your forehead in an open-handed, palm forward salute. (8) Then, lower your left hand to your left side and return to your original position.

KIHON (BASICS I)

Kihon or *Basics I* presents the most elementary levels of *Uchi-Kata* (striking), *Tsuki-Kata* (poking or thrusting) and *Uke-Kata* (blocking). As used here, these applications and their handwork involve completing a technique with what is fundamentally a single, basic movement of the bo. The only footwork used, if any, are stationary pivots into right and left zenkutsu-dachi positions.

uchi~kata (striking)

UCHI-OTOSHI (Overhead Strike)
Grasp the bo with the jun nigiri (basic hold), right hand uppermost. Assume a right zenkutsu-dachi. Crashing forward and down, use the upper or right section of the bo to deliver a forceful strike to your opponent's head.

UCHI-AGE (Upward Strike)
Use the uchi-age in combination with the uchi-otoshi. After delivering the downward strike to your adversary's head, maintain the jun nigiri hold and pull the upper or right section of the bo back over your left shoulder. At the same time, swiftly shoot the lower section forward and up into your opponent's chin or groin.

MOROTE-UCHI
(Double-Handed Thrust)
Grasp the bo with the gyaku nigiri (reverse hold) and assume a right zenkutsu-dachi. Using both hands to hold the bo in a horizontal position, (1) thrust the staff forward and up into your opponent's chin or throat or (2) slam it down into the back of his neck or head. Hit the target with the center section of the staff held between your hands.

YOSE-NIGIRI-UCHI
(Double Hold Overhead Strike)
Assume a right zenkutsu-dachi. Using the yose nigiri (double hold), right hand leading, hold the bo at one end and position it vertically before you. Swing the staff over your head, then bring it down sharply. Snap the forward end down on your adversary's head.

YOKO-UCHI (Side Strike)

Grasp the bo with the jun nigiri, right hand uppermost. Assume a right zen-kutsu-dachi. Whip the upper or right section of the staff inward from your outside right, (1) striking high to the left side of your opponent's head and face or (2) executing a middle level blow to the left side of his body.

GYAKU-YOKO-UCHI (Reverse Side Strike)

Grasp the bo with the jun nigiri, right hand uppermost. Assume a right zen-kutsu-dachi. Pull the upper or right section of the bo back to your right side. At the same time, thrust the lower or left section of the staff inward, (1) striking high to the right side of your opponent's face and

head or (2) executing a middle level blow to the right side of his body. Rotate your shoulders and hips clockwise (that is, to the right) as you move to put added force behind the blow. Any sequence of yoko-uchi and gyaku-yoko-uchi techniques, to either or both high and middle targets, forms an effective combination.

GEDAN-UCHI or
GEDAN-SOTO-UCHI (Low Strike)

Hold the bo with the jun nigiri, left hand uppermost. For best results, assume a right gyaku-zenkutsu-dachi (rear defense stance) and position the lower section of the staff near your right foot. Use it in a movement from the inside to the outside (from right to left), striking to the inside of your opponent's leading right knee.

GYAKU-GEDAN-UCHI or
GEDAN-UCHI-BARAI
(Reverse Low Strike)

Hold the bo with the jun nigiri, left hand uppermost. Again, assume a right gyaku-zenkutsu-dachi and position the lower section of the staff over your right foot. Moving it from the outside to the inside (from left to right), thrust the lower section to the outside of your adversary's leading right knee.

tsuki~kata (poking or thrusting)

TSUKI-KOMI (Two-Handed Thrust)
Grasp the bo with the jun nigiri, right hand uppermost, and assume a right zenkutsu-dachi. Use both hands to stab the upper or right end of the staff horizontally into your adversary's solar plexus.

GYAKU-ZUKI (Reverse Thrust)
Grasp the bo with the jun nigiri, right hand uppermost, and assume a right zenkutsu-dachi. Rotating your shoulders and hips clockwise, pull the upper or right section of the bo horizontally over your right shoulder. Shoot the lower or left end of the staff into your opponent's face.

NAGASHI-ZUKI (Sliding Thrust)

Grasp the bo with the jun nigiri, right hand uppermost, and assume a right zenkutsu-dachi. Position the bo on your left side, its right or upper end leading. With a smooth, even movement of your left hand, slide it swiftly through your right hand into your opponent's chin. Then, before the bo slides through completely, secure your grip and push farther into the target.

TSUKI-OTOSHI
(Reverse Downward Thrust)

(1) Hold the bo easily but securely with both hands, spreading them, palms toward the floor, about two and one-half shoulder-widths apart. Assume a right gyaku-zenkutsu-dachi. Angle the bo over your right leg, its left end held high, its right end aimed at your opponent's foot. (2) Push down firmly with your left hand. Use your right to guide the staff and fire the bo into the target.

uke ~kata (blocking)

MOROTE-UKE, UPWARD
(Double-Handed Block)
Use the upward morote-uke to counter uchi-otoshi (overhead strike) attacks. As your adversary's staff comes down, grasp your bo with the gyaku nigiri and assume a right zenkutsu-dachi. Forcefully thrust your bo upward, catching the on-coming weapon with the center section of your own.

MOROTE-UKE, DOWNWARD
(Double-Handed Block)
Use the downward morote-uke to counter uchi-age (upward strike) attempts. As your opponent's strike approaches, grasp your bo with the gyaku nigiri and assume a right zenkutsu-dachi. Bring your bo straight down, hitting your adversary's weapon perpendicularly. As before, catch the attacking weapon with the center section of your staff.

MOROTE-UKE, SIDEWAYS
(Double-Handed Block)
Use the sideways morote-uke against yoko-uchi (side strike) attacks. To counter an attack from the left, shift back into a right kokutsu-dachi (back stance). Simultaneously, move into a hasami nigiri (palm hold), left hand uppermost, and position your weapon vertically. As the blow approaches, block by sliding your bo firmly to the left.

MOROTE-UKE, BACKWARDS
(Double-Handed Block)
Also use the backward morote-uke against yoko-uchi attempts. To counter an attack from the left, shift back and pivot into a right gyaku-zenkutsu-dachi. Quickly turn your torso clockwise to face toward your opponent. Hold the bo, your left hand uppermost, with either the gyaku nigiri, as shown, or the hasami nigiri, as in the sideways morote-uke. Angle your weapon as you block your opponent's staff with the center section of your own.

YOKO-UKE
(Inside to Outside Block)
Grasp your bo with the jun nigiri, right hand uppermost, and assume a right zenkutsu-dachi. Deflect an attack from the right by moving the upper section of your bo from the inside to the outside (that is, from left to right).

YOKO-UKE
(Outside to Inside Block)
Grasp your bo with the jun nigiri, right hand uppermost, and assume a right zenkutsu-dachi. Deflect your opponent's attack from the left by moving the upper section of your bo from the outside to the inside (that is, from right to left). This technique is also called the *yoko-uchi-uke* because it involves a simultaneous blocking/striking motion.

AGE-UKE (Upper Side Block)
Use the age-uke against overhead blows. Grasp the bo with the gyaku nigiri. As your opponent's strike approaches from the left, pivot counterclockwise 90 degrees into a left zenkutsu-dachi. Simultaneously, angle the right section of your bo upward and inward (to your left) to block your adversary's staff.

GYAKU-AGE-UKE
(Reverse Upper Side Block)
Use the gyaku-age-uke against overhead blows also. Grasp the bo with the gyaku nigiri. As your opponent's strike approaches from the right, pivot clockwise 90 degrees into a right zenkutsu-dachi. Simultaneously, angle the left section of your bo upward and inward (in this case, to your right) to block your adversary's staff.

HARAI-UKE (Lower Side Block or Downward Block)

Use the harai-uke against low attacks. To counter a strike approaching from the low left, grasp the bo with the jun nigiri, right hand uppermost. Pivot counterclockwise 90 degrees into a left zenkutsu-dachi. Simultaneously, push the upper or right end of the bo downward, moving it from the outside to the inside (that is, from right to left) to block the attack.

GYAKU-HARAI-UKE (Reverse Lower Side Block or Reverse Downward Block)

Use the gyaku-harai-uke against low attacks also. To counter a strike approaching from the low left, grasp the bo with the jun nigiri, left hand uppermost. Pivot clockwise 45 degrees into a right zenkutsu-dachi. Simultaneously, begin rotating the bo clockwise around its center, turning your right palm toward the ceiling, your left palm toward the floor. Then, pull the right or lower end under your left arm and hold the bo horizontally against your left side. Bring the left or upper section of the weapon forward and down, moving it from the inside to the outside (that is, from right to left) to block the attack.

KOTEI KIHON (BASICS II)

Kotei Kihon or *Basics II* presents several basic techniques and a series of techniques in combination. The basic techniques here, blocking movements a shade more complex than those presented in Basics I, gradually lead up to rather involved, twirling, flipping, blocking and striking combinations. The minimal footwork used in this section consists of very simple pivots and steps either forward or back. While performing these exercises, try to develop good hand/eye coordination and remember that effective, solidly-executed bo-jitsu movements require constant study.

In practice, many of kobu-do's basic movements are very similar to those found in karate. As such, your prior knowledge of karate may cause the bo-jitsu stances, blocks and strikes to appear easy. Do not be deceived into believing this is so. Mastery of kobu-do demands many years of diligent, dedicated and patient training in the basics as well as the more advanced flipping and twirling maneuvers.

basic blocks

HARAI-UKE (Downward Block)
(1) Begin in a soto-hachiji-dachi (natural stance). Hold the bo across your body with the jun nigiri (basic hold), right hand uppermost. (2) As you use both hands to raise the staff to an angled position before you, right end toward the ceiling, (3) begin moving the bo in a counterclockwise rotation. Push the upper (or right) section to the left and down with your right hand; the lower (or left) section to the right and up, with your left. (4) Continue the rotation, crossing your right arm over your

left, until the bo lies horizontally across your body. (5) Laterally, moving the bo to your right side, position what is now the rear section of the staff behind your right shoulder. Tuck your left hand under your right armpit. Block by using your right hand to push the forward section of the weapon to the outside (that is, to the right).

During practice, remember to use strong wrist and shoulder movements as they insure adequate power and proper technique.

YOKO-UKE
(Inside to Outside Block)
(1) Begin in a soto-hachiji-dachi (natural stance). Hold the bo across your body with the jun nigiri (basic hold), right hand uppermost. (2-3) Begin rotating your hips and shoulders to the left in a counter-clockwise turn. At the same time, use both hands to bring the bo horizon-

tally over to the left side of your body (the inside position). (4) Then, with your right hand, swing the forward section of the staff upward. (5) Keeping your torso turned to the left, block an attack from the right by pulling the forward section of the weapon back toward your outside (that is, to the right).

YOKO-UCHI-UKE
(Outside to Inside Block)

(1) Assume a soto-hachiji-dachi (natural stance) and grasp the bo with the jun nigiri (basic hold), right hand uppermost. Raise the staff over your right shoulder (the outside), positioning what was initially the right end of the weapon to the rear. (2) Using strong wrist actions, snap the bo forward and down, angling the lower section toward your left hip, the upper section toward your right shoulder. (3) Smoothly swing the staff, still angled, across your chest and toward the left side of your body. (4) Simultaneously strike and block by pushing the upper section of the bo to the inside (that is, farther to the left).

TATE-UKE (Vertical Block)

(1) Assume a soto-hachiji-dachi (natural stance) and hold the bo across your body with the jun nigiri (basic hold), right hand uppermost. Move the bo counterclockwise into a vertical position directly before you, your right hand on top and even with your forehead. (2-3) Using both hands to reverse the movement, rotate the weapon clockwise 180 degrees. Block with the center section as the staff enters a vertical position with your left hand on top.

kotei kihon combinations

**YOKO-UCHI/GYAKU-YOKO-UCHI
(Side Snap Strike/Reverse Strike)**
(1) To deliver the yoko-uchi, assume
a left gyaku-zenkutsu-dachi (rear defense stance) and grasp the bo with
the jun nigiri (basic hold), right hand
uppermost. Again, raise the staff over
your right shoulder, positioning what
was initially the right end of the
weapon to the rear. (2-3) Pivot on
both feet and turn yourself counterclockwise 45 degrees into a left zenkutsu-dachi (forward stance). At the
same time, use both hands to swing

the bo forward, down and around to the left. (4) Pulling the left section of the weapon over toward your left side, strike the right section horizontally into your opponent's solar plexus. (5-6) To begin the gyaku-yokouchi, reverse your arm movements. Pull the right section of the bo back toward your right side and, (7) with a strong, pushing movement, shoot the left section horizontally into your adversary's solar plexus.

TATE-UCHI/GYAKU-TATE-UCHI
(Overhead Strike/Reverse Strike)

(1) To deliver the tate-uchi (overhead strike), assume a right zenkutsu-dachi (forward stance) and grasp the bo with the jun nigiri (basic hold), right hand uppermost. Raise the staff over your right shoulder as in the yoko-uchi-uke, positioning what was initially the right end of the weapon to the rear. (2) Swing the bo forward and down, angling the lower section toward your left hip, the upper section near your right shoulder.

(3) Pull the lower section horizontally over to your left side and (4) forcefully snap the upper section downward into the target. (5) Bring the staff back to a horizontal position to begin the gyku-tate-uchi. (6-7) Smoothly raise the forward section of the weapon over your right shoulder and, (8) with a strong, pushing movement, shoot the other section up through your opponent's chin.

GYAKU-UCHI-AGE/UCHI-OTOSHI
(Reverse Strike/Overhead Strike)

(1) To deliver the gyaku-uchi-age, assume a right zenkutsu-dachi (forward stance) and grasp the bo with the jun nigiri (basic hold), right palm toward the ceiling. Hold the staff horizontally under your left arm and against the left side of your body. Position what was initially the left side of the weapon to the rear. (2) Using both hands, begin rotating the rear section of the weapon down, forward and up, the forward section up, backward and down. (3) Continue the rotation, simultaneously raising the staff hori-

zontally over your left shoulder. (4) To block, shoot what is now the forward end of the bo up through your opponent's chin with a strong pushing motion. (5) To complete the combination, reverse your arm movements, rotating the section now held over your left shoulder up, forward and down, the other section down, backward and up. (6-7) As you follow through with this second rotation, lower the staff to your left side. Then, using both hands, bring what is now the forward section down in a snappy uchi-otoshi (overhead strike).

ICHIMONJI-MAWASHI
(Overhead Twirl into a Side Strike)

(1) Assume a right zenkutsu-dachi (forward stance) and grasp the bo with the jun nigiri (basic hold), right palm toward the ceiling. Then, flip the staff over to a horizontal position on your right side. Extend your right hand before you, palm toward the floor, and tuck your left hand, palm toward the ceiling, under your right arm. (2-3) To deliver the ichimonji-mawashi, begin moving the bo to the left laterally. Simultaneously, begin a 180-degree counterclockwise pivot into a left zenkutsu-dachi. Pull up and back with your right hand and push forward and out with your left to begin the staff's clockwise overhead twirl. (4) To accommodate the twirl, slip the forefingers of both hands around the shaft, holding it between your fore- and middle fingers. As you approach a 90-degree pivot, angle the staff overhead. Pass your right hand, palm facing away, above your forehead as your left hand, palm toward you, moves before you on a level slightly below it. (5-6) Twirl the staff clockwise 180 degrees, passing your left hand, palm facing away, above your forehead as your right hand, palm toward you, moves before you on a level slightly below that. (7-8) Now, push forward and out with your left hand and pull backward and in with your right, flipping the bo into a horizontal position on your left side. Extend your left hand before you, palm toward the floor, and tuck your right hand, palm toward the ceiling, under your left arm. (9) Smoothly move the bo farther to the left to deliver a strong, forceful yoko-uchi (side strike).

For maximum proficiency, concentrate on using smooth, even movements throughout and practice the technique both to the left and to the right.

MAE-MAWASHI
(Overhead Twirl into a Downward Side Strike)

(1) Assume a right zenkutsu-dachi (forward stance). Execute a right harai-uke (downward block), ending with the bo held on your right side, your left hand tucked under your right armpit. (2-3) Rotate the bo in a clockwise overhead twirl, as in the ichimonji-mawashi, but do not pivot out of the right zenkutsu-dachi. The mae-mawashi differs from the ichimonji-mawashi in that the feet are kept stationary throughout. As you move the bo to the left laterally, pull it up and back with your right hand and push forward and out with your left. Again, to accommodate the twirl, slip the forefingers of both hands around the shaft, holding it between your fore- and middle fingers. (4) Continue the rotation so that as your right hand, palm facing away, passes above your forehead, your left hand, palm toward you, moves before you on a level slightly below it. (5-6) Twirl the staff clockwise 180 degrees, passing your left hand, palm facing away, above your forehead as your right, palm toward you, moves before you on a level slightly below it. (7-8) Now, push forward and out with your left hand and pull backward and in with your right, flipping the bo into a horizontal position on your left side. Extend your left hand before you, palm toward the floor, and tuck your right hand, palm toward the ceiling, under your left arm. (9) Smoothly move the bo downward and farther to the left to deliver a strong, forceful strike.

HACHIJI-MAWASHI
("Figure Eight" Movement)

(1) Assume a soto-hachiji-dachi (natural stance) and grasp the bo with the hasami nigiri (palm hold), left hand uppermost. Angle the bo over on the right side of your body with your left hand forward, your right hand nearest the ground. (2) Using both arms, trace a "figure eight" with the weapon: With the staff still on your right side, rotate the bo counterclockwise, pushing straight down with your left hand and up with your right. (3-4) As your right arm comes up, cross it over your left. Then, push downward with your right hand and up with your left to angle the bo toward the low left. (5) Turn your body counterclockwise (that is, to the left). Simultaneously, rotate the bo clockwise. Pull straight up with your right hand and down with your left. (6-7) Continue the clockwise rotation until the bo enters a head-level horizontal position with your right hand forward. (8) Now, turn your body clockwise (that is, to the right). Continue the bo's clockwise rotation. Pull down with your right hand and up with your left to angle the weapon toward the low right. (9) End the movement by bringing the bo over to your right side, left hand forward, right hand nearest the ground, as at the start.

OSAE-UKE
(Bar or Pinning Maneuver)
(1) Assume a soto-hachiji-dachi (natural stance). Using the jun nigiri (basic hold), angle the bo across your body, right hand uppermost. (2) Step forward with your left foot, (3-4) pivoting clockwise into a left

gyaku-zenkutsu-dachi (rear defense stance). As you pivot, bring the left section of the weapon down and around in a clockwise sweep over your left foot. (5) Firmly push the left end of the staff into the target to deliver the pinning action.

KATA-SUKASHI
(Under-Arm Grip)

(1) Assume a soto-hachiji-dachi (natural stance). Keep your arms along your sides. With your right hand, knuckles to the outside, grasping it slightly above its center, hold the bo vertically behind your right arm and shoulder. (2) Swing your right hand forward and up, (3) bringing the weapon to a vertical position in front of your right shoulder. Place the back of your open left hand behind the lower section of the staff. Push with it to help (4) flip the bo over into an upright position behind your right shoulder. Slip your left hand under your right arm (5) to catch the shaft. (6) Release the hold of your right hand. Use your left, palm toward the floor, to pull the bo forward horizontally. (7) Slide the bo over to your left side. Simultaneously, rotate it clockwise 90 degrees (8) into a vertical position in front of your left shoulder. (9) Now, as you raise your left arm, twist your left wrist counterclockwise to rotate the bo 180 degrees. (10-11) Flip the staff over into an upright position behind your left shoulder. (12) Bring your right hand across and slip it under your left arm to catch the shaft.

Smooth movement, correct distance and proper timing are essential for the proper execution of this technique.

USHIRO-DORI (Back Grab)

(1) Assume a soto-hachiji-dachi (natural stance). With your right hand, palm toward the floor, grasping it securely a little to the right of center, hold the bo horizontally before you. Your left hand may help to bring it to this position but remove it once the technique begins. (2) As you pivot clockwise 45 degrees into a right zenkutsu-dachi (forward stance), swing the weapon forward in a clockwise sweep, (3-4) moving it up, over and behind your right shoulder. Simultaneously, begin reaching back at waist level with your left hand. (5) Angle the staff across your back, the lower end toward your left hip, (6) and catch it from the inside with your left hand. (7) Release the hold of your right hand. (8-9) Use your left hand to sweep the bo down, around and forward in a clockwise movement. At the same time, twist your wrist counterclockwise to (10) bring the staff into an upright position in front of your left shoulder. (11) Now, as you pivot counterclockwise 45 degrees into a left zenkutsu-dachi, move the staff up, over and behind your left shoulder. Angle it across your back, the lower end toward your right hip. Begin reaching back at waist level with your right hand and (12) catch the bo from the inside.

DAISHA-MAWASHI
(Large Circular Movement)

(1) Assume a soto-hachiji-dachi (natural stance). Using the jun nigiri (basic hold), right palm toward the ceiling, hold the bo horizontally across your body. Then, raise the weapon before you to a level even with your eyes. (2-6) Now, release the hold of your left hand. Using your right hand as a fulcrum, begin a 360-degree counterclockwise rotation of the staff. At the same time, move your right arm out, around and back in a 180-degree downward, clockwise sweep. Coincide completion of the staff's rotation with the completion of your arm's lateral sweep. As the bo moves, pivot counterclockwise into a left zenkutsu-dachi (forward stance). Lean forward slightly to accommodate these actions. (7) At this point, your right hand, palm toward the ceiling, should be holding the bo horizontally behind your lower back. Smoothly slide the staff toward your left hip and reach back with your left hand to catch it in an under-hand grip. At the same time, pivot clockwise into a right zenkutsu-dachi. (8-11) Release the hold of your right hand. Now, using your left hand as a fulcrum, begin a 180-degree counterclockwise rotation of the bo. Simultaneously, move your left arm out, around and forward in a 180-degree upward, clockwise sweep. Coincide completion of the weapon's rotation with the completion of your arm's lateral sweep. (12) As the bo moves before you, angle the palm of your left hand toward the floor. Raise your right hand, palm angled toward the ceiling, to catch the staff with the jun nigiri (basic hold).

As before, smooth movement and good hand-eye coordination are essential to this type of rotating technique.

IDO~KIHON (BASICS III)

The next phase in training is known as *Ido-Kihon* or *Basics III*. The movements here, as opposed to those covered in the Kotei Kihon section, involve coordinating hand manipulations with a fair amount of footwork. Again, the section begins with several techniques basic to this level, then gradually builds up to a series of complicated combinations.

To properly execute these advanced Ido-Kihon techniques, you must consider and fuse together three essential elements:

(1) Balance and a Low Center of Gravity

You must have good balance and good form to complete smooth, properly executed techniques. Strong stances will give you the solid foundation necessary to achieve both. For a strong stance, you must maintain a center of gravity low enough to preserve stability, yet high enough to leave mobility in all directions unimpaired. A low but comfortable stance that allows easy mobility is the best for practicing Ido-Kihon.

(2) Power and Speed

The proper relationship between power and speed must be learned well for the effective use and control of both. While power is not necessarily required for speed, speed is essential to good power. If your techniques lack speed, your power will suffer and, by consequence, your kobu-do progress will slacken. So, work on building up speed. However, if your executions lack power, speed is useless. So, to help increase power, use large movements—particularly in the execution of striking techniques. To help control your power, learn to use *kime*, the process of focusing all mental and physical energies on the task at hand. Practically speaking, this means tensing your muscles only at the moment of impact.

(3) Rhythm and Timing

An internal feeling for the rhythm of movements will sharpen your use of both faster and slower techniques. It will also help your timing. With poor timing, any technique—regardless of its potential strength—will prove ineffective. You must learn to execute techniques at the proper moment. Your movements must be timed accurately, neither too fast, too slow, too close nor too far away.

basic techniques

HIDARI-NO-KAMAE (Stepping Forward with Your Right Foot)

(1) Assume a musubi-dachi (ready stance). With your right hand, hold the bo vertically in front of your right arm and shoulder. (2) Turning counterclockwise 45 degrees, pivot into a left sanchin-dachi (tension stance). (3) Simultaneously, bring your left hand up, palm forward, into the yoi (ready) position. (4-6) Now, begin stepping forward 45 degrees with your right foot into a right zenkutsu-dachi (forward stance). Pulling forward and down with your left hand and pushing upward and back with your right, move the bo into a horizontal position at your right side. Twist your right hand clockwise around the shaft so that your right palm faces the ceiling. Raise the weapon over your right shoulder in readiness for an uchi-otoshi (overhead strike). (7) As you come down into the zenkutsu-dachi, drop what is now the forward section of the staff down and over to your left side. (8) Forcefully snap the other end forward and down into the target.

In this instance, execute the hidari-no-kamae (which protects your left flank) by stepping forward with your right foot into a right zenkutsu-dachi.

HIDARI-NO-KAMAE
(Stepping Back with Your Left Foot)
(1) Assume a musubi-dachi (ready stance). With your right hand, hold the bo vertically in front of your right arm and shoulder. (2) Turning counterclockwise 45 degrees, pivot into a left sanchin-dachi (tension stance). (3) Simultaneously, bring your left hand up, palm forward, into the yoi (ready) position. (4) Now, pivot clockwise on your right foot and step back 45 degrees with your left into a right zenkutsu-dachi (forward stance). (5-6) Pulling forward and down with your left hand and pushing upward and back with your right, move the bo into a horizontal position at your right side. Twist your right hand clockwise around the shaft so that your right palm faces the ceiling. Raise the weapon over your right shoulder in

92

readiness for an uchi-otoshi (over-head strike). (7) Then, drop what is now the forward section of the staff down and over to your left side. (8) Forcefully snap the other end forward and down into the target.

Here, you execute the hidari-no-kamae by stepping backward with your left foot. However, whether you step back with your left foot or forward with your right to assume the right zenkutsu-dachi, the hidari-no-kamae protects your left flank.

To execute the migi-no-kamae which protects your right flank, either step forward with your left foot or back with your right to assume a left zen-kutsu-dachi. Accordingly, adjust the movements of your hands, position-ing the weapon on your right side as it comes down to strike the target.

TSUKI (Thrusting)

(1) Assume a right zenkutsu-dachi (forward stance). Using the jun nigiri (basic hold), right hand uppermost and leading, hold the bo angled forward at your left side. (2) Deliver a strong, backward thrust to the rear left. (3-4) Then, with both hands, shoot the staff forward in a tsuki-komi (two-handed thrust) to your opponent's midsection. (5-7) Begin moving your left foot forward into a left zenkutsu-dachi. Pull the forward section of the bo upward, bringing the staff to a vertical position before you. At the same time, reverse the placement of your hands by sliding your right hand down the shaft as your left hand moves up past it. (8) Grasp the weapon securely with the jun nigiri, left hand uppermost and leading, and angle the staff at your right side. (9) Now, as you come down into the left zenkutsu-dachi, deliver a strong, backward thrust to the rear right. (10) Then, with both hands, again shoot the staff forward in a tsuki-komi to your opponent's midsection.

SUKUIAGE SUNAKAKE
(Sweeping)

(1) Assume a right zenkutsu-dachi (forward stance). Hold the bo angled forward on your left side with the jun nigiri (basic hold), right palm toward the ceiling. (2) Move your right hand, palm toward the floor, into a hasami nigiri (palm hold) over the shaft. (3) Begin stepping forward with your left foot into a left zenkutsu-dachi. Rotate the bo, sweeping the rear section forward, downward and up. (4) As the bo moves, turn your left wrist counter-clockwise and slip your hand around the shaft into a hasami nigiri, palm toward the ceiling. (5) With your right hand, push the staff down past your right shoulder. As you step into the left zenkutsu-dachi, angle the bo forward on your right side. Ease your hands into the jun nigiri, left palm toward the ceiling. (6-7) Move your left hand, palm toward the floor, into a hasami nigiri over the shaft. (8) Begin stepping forward with your right foot into a right zenkutsu-dachi. (9) Rotate the bo, sweeping what is now the rear section forward, downward and up. As the bo moves, turn your right wrist clockwise and slip your hand around the shaft into a hasami nigiri, palm toward the ceiling. (10) With your left hand, push the staff down past your left shoulder. (11) As you step into the right zenkutsu-dachi, angle the bo forward on your left side. Ease your hands into the jun nigiri, right palm toward the ceiling.

The early bo-jitsu fighter used this technique to blind and distract his adversary. As the bo rotated, he would sweep the lower end of the staff forward, down along the ground, then swiftly upward, scooping sand and dirt into the face and eyes of his opponent.

UCHI-OTOSHI (Overhead Strike)

(1) Assume a left zenkutsu-dachi (forward stance). Hold the bo with the jun nigiri (basic hold), right palm toward the ceiling. Angle the weapon over on your right side, left hand uppermost and leading. (2) Raise the staff to a horizontal position over your right shoulder. (3-4) Then, using both hands, bring the forward section of the staff down to your left side. Forcefully thrust the other end forward and down in a powerful right uchi-otoshi (overhead strike).

(5-6) Swiftly take your right hand out of the jun nigiri and grasp the bo from the outside (that is, from the right) with the basic grip, palm toward the floor. (7-8) Then, take your open left hand and place it under the staff, palm toward the ceiling. Grasp the weapon securely. Push what is now the rear end upward and raise the bo over your left shoulder, your right hand now leading. At the same time, step forward with your left foot into a left zenkutsu-dachi. (9-10) Bring what is now the forward section of the staff down to your right side and thrust the other end forward and down in a left uchi-otoshi (overhead strike).

YOKO-UCHI (Side Striking)

(1) Assume a right kiba-dachi (horse stance). Hold the bo horizontally across your body with the gyaku ni-giri (reverse hold). (2-4) Pivoting clockwise 180 degrees on your right foot, slide your left foot forward and around into a left kiba-dachi. Simultaneously, use both hands to bring the bo around laterally in a clockwise sweep. (5) Forcefully thrust out the left section of the staff in a snappy yoko-uchi (side strike). (6-8) Now, pivoting counterclockwise 180 degrees on your left foot, slide your right foot forward and around in a right kiba-dachi. Simultaneously, use both hands to bring the bo around laterally in a counterclockwise sweep. (9) Forcefully thrust out the right section of the staff in a snappy yoko-uchi (side strike).

To maintain a solid kiba-dachi and to insure proper execution of your yoko-uchi, take smooth, even steps and always keep your center of gravity low.

MAE-UKE FROM A KOKUTSU-DACHI
(Vertical Block from a Back Stance)
(1) Assume a right zenkutsu-dachi (forward stance). Using the jun nigiri (basic hold), right hand uppermost and leading, hold the bo angled forward at your left side. (2) Keep most of your weight on your right leg as you begin sliding your left forward into a left kokutsu-dachi (back stance). Simultaneously, push the staff down and forward with your left hand; pull it up and back with your right. (3-4) As your left hand pushes outward, twist your left wrist counterclockwise and slip your hand out of the jun nigiri into a hasami nigiri (palm hold), palm toward the ceiling. Block firmly as your right hand, palm toward you, nears forehead level and the bo moves through a vertical position before you.

(5) Now, smoothly begin a clockwise rotation of the staff. With your right hand, pull it toward your right shoulder. With your left, push it up and out. As your left hand pushes, twist your left wrist clockwise, slipping your hand out of the hasami nigiri, palm toward the ceiling, into a hasami nigiri, palm toward the floor. At the same time, keep most of your weight on your left leg and begin sliding your right forward into a right kokutsu-dachi. (6) Continue the clockwise rotation. Use your right hand to pull the staff down past your right shoulder. Use your left hand to push it up past your left shoulder. (7) Block as your left hand, palm away from you, nears forehead level and the bo moves through a vertical position before you.

MAE-UKE FROM A
NEKOASHI-DACHI
(Vertical Block from a Cat Stance)

(1) Assume a right zenkutsu-dachi (forward stance). Using the jun nigiri (basic hold), right hand uppermost and leading, hold the bo angled forward at your left side. (2) Keep most of your weight on your right leg as you begin sliding your left forward into a left nekoashi-dachi (cat stance). Simultaneously, push the staff down and forward with your left hand; pull it up and back with your right. (3-4) As your left hand pushes outward, twist your left wrist counterclockwise and slip your hand out of the jun nigiri into a hasami nigiri (palm hold), palm toward the ceiling. Block firmly as your right hand, palm toward you, nears forehead level and the bo moves through a vertical position before you. (5) Now, begin a smooth clockwise rotation of the staff, pulling it toward your right shoulder with your right hand and pushing it up and out

with your left. As your right hand pulls, twist your right wrist counterclockwise into a hasami nigiri, palm toward the floor. As your left hand pushes, twist your left wrist clockwise into a hasami nigiri, palm toward the floor also. At the same time, keep most of your weight on your left leg and begin sliding your right foot forward into a right neko-ashi-dachi. (6) Continue the rotation, bringing the bo horizontally before you at eye level. (7) Then, use your right hand to pull the shaft down past your right shoulder, your left hand to push it up past your left shoulder. Block as your left hand, palm away from you, nears forehead level and the bo moves through a vertical position before you.

The movements here and those of executing a mae-uke from the kokutsu-dachi are basically the same. They differ only in the stance assumed.

HARAI-UKE
(Downward Block)

(1) Assume a right zenkutsu-dachi (forward stance). Hold the bo angled forward on your left side with the jun nigiri (basic hold), right palm toward the ceiling. (2-3) With your right hand, palm toward the floor, catch the bo with the basic grip. (4) With your open left hand, push the staff upward. Simultaneously, begin stepping forward with your left foot into a left zenkutsu-dachi. (5) Raise the weapon over your head, rotating it clockwise. (6) Continue the rotation, crossing your left arm over your right. Begin lowering the staff so that your right hand approaches your left side and your left hand passes your right shoulder. (7) As your left foot comes down into the left zenkutsu-dachi, position the bo horizontally against your left side. Tuck your right hand under your left armpit and complete the left harai-uke. (8) Begin stepping forward with your right foot into a right zenkutsu-dachi. (9) Raise the bo above your head. Manipulate your fingers so that the weapon is held between the fore- and middle fingers of each hand, palms facing each other. (10) Begin a counterclockwise rotation of the bo, (11) crossing your right arm over your left. Simultaneously, begin lowering the staff so that your left hand approaches your right side and your right hand nears your left shoulder. (12) As your right foot comes down into the right zenkutsu-dachi, position the bo horizontally against your right side. Tuck your left hand under your right armpit and complete the right harai-uke.

YOKO-UKE
(Inside to Outside Block)

(1) Assume a right zenkutsu-dachi (forward stance). Using the jun nigiri, right hand uppermost and leading, hold the bo angled forward at your left side. (2) Begin stepping forward with your left foot into a left zenkutsu-dachi. (3-4) Bring the bo around in a clockwise sweep, pulling to the right and back with your right hand, pushing forward and out with your left. (5) Simultaneously, manipulate your hands into a jun nigiri, this time with your right palm toward the floor, your left palm toward the ceiling. As you come down into the left zenkutsu-dachi, position the staff horizontally against your right side (the inside position). (6) Then, with your left hand, swing what is now the forward section of the weapon upward. (7) Execute a strong, well-focused left yoko-uke by pulling the bo back toward your outside (that is, to the left). (8-10) Now, step forward with your right foot into a right zenkutsu-dachi. Bring the bo around in a counterclockwise sweep, pushing forward with your right hand, pulling back and to the left with your left hand. Simultaneously, manipulate your hands into a jun nigiri with the palm of your left hand facing the floor, the palm of your right hand facing the ceiling. (11) Position the staff horizontally against your left side (in this particular case, the inside). (12) Then, swing the bo upward and pull it back toward your outside (in this case, toward the right) to deliver the right yoko-uke.

NANAME-AGE-UCHI
(Diagonal Side Strike to the Face)

(1) Assume a right zenkutsu-dachi (forward stance). Using the gyaku nigiri (reverse hold), hold the bo angled across your body, right hand uppermost. (2) Begin stepping forward with your left foot into a left zenkutsu-dachi. (3) Simultaneously, bring the bo forward and around in a lateral clockwise sweep. (4) As you come down into the left zenkutsu-dachi, angle the staff over to your right side. With your left hand uppermost and leading, firmly thrust what is now the forward section of the

weapon into the left side of your opponent's face. (5) Now, begin stepping forward with your right foot into a right zenkutsu-dachi. (6) Simultaneously, bring the bo forward and around in a lateral counterclockwise sweep. (7) As you come down into the right zenkutsu-dachi, angle the staff over to your left side. With your right hand uppermost and leading, firmly thrust what is now the forward section of the weapon into the right side of your opponent's face.

OSAE-UKE (Pinning)

(1) Assume a right zenkutsu-dachi (forward stance). Using the jun nigiri, right hand uppermost and leading, hold the bo angled forward at your left side. (2) As you step forward with your left foot, (3-4) pivot clockwise on your right into a left gyaku-zenkutsu-dachi (rear defense stance). Simultaneously, bring the lower section of the weapon down and around in a clockwise sweep over your left foot. (5) Then, by firmly pushing the lower section of the staff into the target, deliver the osae-uke. (6-8) Step forward with your right foot. Take your right hand out of the jun nigiri and, grasping the bo with your right palm toward the floor, move into a gyaku nigiri (reverse hold). Push down with your right hand to angle the staff forward at your right side, left hand uppermost and leading. (9) Pivot counterclockwise into a right gyaku-zenkutsu-dachi. Simultaneously, bring what is now the lower section of the weapon down and around in a counterclockwise sweep over your right foot. (10) Firmly push the lower section of the staff into the target to deliver the second osae-uke.

ido kihon combinations

The following sequences exemplify effective combinations of techniques. Feel free to experiment with any combination you desire but remember to execute all movements correctly for maximum proficiency.

HARAI-UKE-TSUKI (Downward Block with a Forward Thrust)
(1) Assume a right zenkutsu-dachi. Using the jun nigiri, right hand uppermost and leading, hold the bo angled forward at your left side. (2-3) Begin stepping forward with your left foot into a left zenkutsu-dachi. Take your right hand out of the jun nigiri and, moving it in from the outside, catch the bo with the basic grip, palm toward the floor. Place your open left hand, palm toward the ceiling, under the staff. Then, use both hands to raise the weapon above your head. (4) Rotate the staff clockwise, crossing your left arm over your right. At the same time, begin lowering the weapon before you. (5) As your left foot comes down into the left zenkutsu-dachi, use your right hand, palm toward the ceiling, to position the bo horizontally against your left side. Tuck your right hand under your left armpit. Complete the left harai-uke by using your left hand, palm toward the floor, to push what is now the forward section of the bo to the outside (that is, to the left). (6-7) Swing the forward section of the bo inward slightly and upward. Push the rear section outward and bring the bo to a vertical position before you, left hand uppermost. (8-9) With both hands, smoothly sweep the weapon down and back horizontally on your right side. (10) Then, with your left

CONTINUED

10

12

hand leading, thrust the staff forward in a tsuki-komi (two-handed thrust) to your opponent's midsection. (11-12) Begin stepping forward with your right foot into a right zenkutsu-dachi. As you raise the staff above your head, rotate it counterclockwise. Manipulate your hands around the shaft to accommodate the movement. (13) Continue the rotation, crossing your right arm over your left. At the same time, begin lowering the weapon before you. (14) As your right foot comes down into the right zenkutsu-dachi, use your left hand, palm toward the ceiling, to position the bo horizontally against your right side. Tuck your left hand under your right armpit. Complete the right harai-uke by using your right hand, palm toward the floor, to push what is now the forward section of the bo to the outside (in this case, to the right). (15-16) Swing the forward section of the bo inward, push the rear section outward and bring the bo to a vertical position before you, your right hand uppermost. (17-18) With both hands, smoothly sweep the weapon down and back horizontally on your left side. (19) Then, with your right hand leading, thrust the staff forward in a second tsuki-komi to your opponent's midsection.

15

18

HARAI-UKE/HACHIJI-MAWASHI (Downward Block/"Figure Eight" Movement)

(1) Assume a right zenkutsu-dachi. Using the jun nigiri, right hand uppermost and leading, hold the bo angled forward at your left side. (2-3) Take your right hand out of the jun nigiri and, moving it in from the right, catch the bo with the basic grip, palm toward the floor. With your open left hand, palm toward the ceiling, push the staff upward. At the same time, begin stepping forward with your left foot into a left zenkutsu-dachi. Use both hands to raise the weapon over your head. As you do so, grasp it securely and rotate it clockwise, crossing your left arm over your right. (4) Continue the rotation, lowering the staff to a horizontal position against your left side. Tuck your right hand under your left armpit and, as you come down into the left zenkutsu-dachi, complete the left harai-uke. (5-6) Maintain the left zenkutsu-dachi and begin a hachiji-mawashi. Crossing your left arm back over your right, move the bo laterally across your body to the right. (7) Then, with your left hand uppermost, bring it to a vertical position on your right side. (8) Push up with your right hand to bring the staff to a shoulder-high horizontal position with your left palm toward the ceiling, your right palm toward the floor. (9) Pull down with your left hand and push up with your right to angle the bo toward the low left. Simultaneously, swing it over to the left side of your body. (10) Then, with your left hand to the rear and uppermost, sweep the weapon up over your left shoulder. (11-12) Using both hands, drop what is now the forward section of the staff down toward your right hip. Snap the other end forward and down into the target. (13-15) Take your left hand,

CONTINUED

palm toward the floor, and grasp the bo from the left. With your open right hand, palm toward the ceiling, push the staff upward. At the same time, begin stepping forward with your right foot into a right zenkutsu-dachi. Use both hands to raise the weapon over your head. (16) Grasp it securely and rotate the bo counterclockwise, crossing your right arm over your left. (17) As you come down into the right zenkutsu-dachi, lower the staff to a horizontal position against your right side, tuck your left hand under your right armpit and complete a right harai-uke. (18) Maintain the right zenkutsu-dachi and begin a second hachiji-mawashi. Cross your right arm back over your left to move the bo laterally across your body to the left. (19-20) Then, with your right hand uppermost, bring it to a vertical position on your left side. Push up with your left hand, bringing the staff to a shoulder-high horizontal position, your right palm toward the ceiling, your left palm toward the floor. (21) Pull down with your right hand and push up with your left to angle the bo toward the low right. (22) Simultaneously, swing it over to the right side of your body. (23-24) Then, with your right hand to the rear and uppermost, sweep the staff up over your right shoulder. (25) Using both hands, drop what is now the forward section of the staff down toward your left hip. Snap the other end forward and down into the target.

UCHI-OTOSHI/YOKO-UKE
(Overhead Strike/Inside to Outside Block)

(1) Assume a musubi-dachi. Using the yoi (ready) position, your left arm across your face, hold the bo vertically in front of your right arm and shoulder. (2) In reality, the footwork from here through no. 5 is completed in one smooth, jumping-in movement. Step forward with your right foot into a right zenkutsu-dachi. At the same time, rotate the bo on your right side, pushing forward and down with your left hand, pulling upward and back with your right. Move your right hand into the jun nigiri to accommodate the rotation. (3) As you move the staff, angle it above your right shoulder, your right hand uppermost and to the rear. (4-5) Then, using both hands, bring what is now the forward section of the weapon down to your left side. Forcefully thrust the other end forward and down in a powerful uchi-otoshi. Simultaneously, step forward with your left foot into a heiso-ku-dachi. (6-7) Now, move the forward section of the staff before you in a lateral counterclockwise sweep to the inside (that is, to the left). At the same time, step back smoothly on your left foot to resume the right zenkutsu-dachi. (8) Then, snap the forward section of the staff upward and back toward the outside (that is, to the right) to complete a right yoko-uke (inside to outside block). (9-10) Bring the bo down vertically in front of your right arm and shoulder, your left arm held across your face, and return to the yoi (ready) position. Repeat the sequence.

122

MAE-UKE/UCHI-OTOSHI
(Vertical Block/Overhead Strike)

(1) Assume a soto-hachiji-dachi. Using the jun nigiri, left palm toward the ceiling, hold the bo horizontally across your body. (2-3) Begin sliding your left foot forward into a left kokutsu-dachi. At the same time, rotate the staff counterclockwise, pulling up with your right hand, pushing down with your left. Complete a mae-uke by blocking as the bo moves into a vertical position before you with your right hand uppermost. (4-5) Shift your weight to your left leg and assume a left zenkutsu-dachi. Simultaneously, begin a clockwise rotation of the weapon. As it approaches a 180-degree turn, angle it over your left shoulder, your left hand to the rear and uppermost. (6) Using both hands, bring what is now the forward section of the weapon down to your right side. Forcefully thrust the other end forward and down in a strong uchi-otoshi. (7-9) Pull the staff up to a vertical position before you. At the same time, slide your right hand up past your left and your left hand down past your right into another jun nigiri. Step forward with your right foot into a right kokutsu-dachi. (10) Begin a clockwise rotation of the bo, positioning it horizontally before you at head level, your right palm toward the ceiling, your left palm toward the floor. (11) Continue the rotation. Complete another mae-uke by blocking as the staff moves into a vertical position before you with your left hand uppermost. (12-13) Shift your weight to your right leg and assume a right zenkutsu-dachi. Simultaneously, begin a counterclockwise rotation of the bo.

CONTINUED

As it approaches a 180-degree turn, angle it over your right shoulder, your right hand to the rear and uppermost. (14) Using both hands, bring what is now the forward section of the staff down to your left side. Forcefully thrust the other end forward and down in a strong uchi-otoshi.

MOROTE-UKE/NANAME-UCHI
(Double-Handed Blocks/
Diagonal Side Strikes)

(1) Assume a soto-hachiji-dachi. Using the gyaku nigiri, hold the bo across your body. (2-3) Step forward with your left foot into a left zenkutsu-dachi. Simultaneously, use both hands to raise the bo horizontally before you in a strong upward morote-uke. (4-5) Follow-up immediately by using both hands to bring it down horizontally in a strong downward morote-uke. (6-7) Continue to maintain the left zenkutsu-dachi. Pull the left section of the bo down toward your rear left and thrust the right

CONTINUED

section forward and up in a snappy right naname-uchi to your opponent's face. (8-9) Then, pull the right section of the weapon down toward your rear right and swiftly snap the left section forward and up in a left naname-uchi. (10-12) Step forward with your right foot into a right zenkutsu-dachi. Simultaneously, use both hands to raise the bo horizontally before you in a second upward morote-uke. (13-14) Follow-up immediately by using both hands to bring it down horizontally in a second downward morote-uke. (15-16) Continue to maintain the right zenkutsu-dachi. Pull the right section of the staff down toward your rear right and thrust the left section forward and up in a snappy left naname-uchi. (17-18) Then, pull the left section of the bo down toward your rear left and swiftly snap the right section forward and up in a right naname-uchi to your adversary's face.

HARAI-UKE/HACHIJI-MAWASHI/ DAISHA-MAWASHI/TSUKI (Downward Block/"Figure Eight" Movement/Large Circular Movement/ Two-Handed Thrust)

(1) Assume a soto-hachiji-dachi. Hold the bo horizontally across your body with the jun nigiri, right palm toward the ceiling. (2-3) Begin stepping forward with your right foot into a right zenkutsu-dachi. Use both hands to raise the weapon before you. At the same time, move the bo in a counterclockwise rotation, crossing your right arm over your left. (4) As you come down into the right zenkutsu-dachi, lower the staff to a horizontal position against your right side, tuck your left hand under your right armpit and complete a right harai-uke.

(5-7) Maintain the right zenkutsu-dachi and begin a hachiji-mawashi. Crossing your right arm back over your left, move the staff laterally across your body to your left side. At the same time, rotate it clockwise 180 degrees, turning your right palm toward the ceiling, your left palm toward the floor. (8) Pull down with your right hand and push up with your left to angle the bo toward the low right. Simultaneously, swing it over to the right side of your body.

(9) Then, with your right hand to the rear, sweep the weapon up over your right shoulder. (10) Begin a second counterclockwise rotation, pushing forward and to the left with your right hand and pulling backward and to the right with your left. (11) Again, cross your right arm over your left, lower the staff horizontally against your right side and tuck your left hand under your right armpit, returning to the right harai-uke position. (12) Release the hold of your left hand to begin the daisha-mawashi. With your right hand, move the staff out, around and back. Simultaneously, use your right hand as a fulcrum and rotate the bo counterclockwise, bringing it to a vertical position behind you. (13) Reach back

13

with your left hand and grasp the shaft. (14-16) Then, release the hold of your right hand. With your left, swing the staff out, around and forward. As you do so, use your left hand as a fulcrum and rotate the bo counterclockwise, bringing it to a horizontal position before you, your left palm facing the floor. (17-18) Grasp the bo with your right hand, palm toward the ceiling. Then, with both hands, continue the weapon's counterclockwise rotation. Again, cross your right arm over your left. (19) Lower the staff to a horizontal position against your right side and tuck your left hand under your right armpit, resuming the right harai-uke. (20-21) Crossing your right arm back over your left, move the staff laterally to a horizontal position across your body. (22) Now, rotate the bo clockwise 90 degrees, pulling up and to the right with your right hand, down and to the left with your left hand to bring it to a vertical position before you. (23-24) Slide the weapon into a horizontal position on your left side, your left hand to the rear. (25) Thrust what is now the forward end out in a tsuki-komi to your opponent's midsection.

16

19

22

23

SELF~DEFENSE
APPLICATIONS
(SPARRING)

The self-defense applications or sparring exercises presented here consist of both unarmed and armed counters to several bo-jitsu techniques. Effective performance of these exercises depends on a fundamental understanding of the basics taught in Kihon, Kotei-Kihon and Ido-Kihon, and requires proper integration of balance, mobility, fluid movement, speed, power, timing and rhythm.

Two elements vital to the successful application of these counters, both in practice and actual sparring situations, are *kime* and *mushin*. *Kime*, as discussed earlier, is the focusing of all mental and physical energies on the situation at hand. *Mushin*, a relaxed state of no-mindedness in which your thoughts are free from the interference of superfluous clutter, allows instinctive action to take command. The hand-in-hand development of kime and mushin will provide you with instinctively faster, more effective responses in almost any kobu-do sparring session.

In order for your instinctive actions to be effective, however, you must vigorously and repeatedly train yourself to react correctly (that is, with good posture, proper stances, smooth. movements, a balanced combination of power and speed, etcetera) and with the appropriate kind of technique. The exercises here (and the kata that follows) are good methods for beginning this type of training. Practice them often, paying particular attention to kime and mushin. Remember also, stay relaxed. Any excess tension will interfere with your mushin.

UNARMED COUNTER TO AN UCHI-OTOSHI (Overhead Strike)

(1-2) As your opponent's right uchi-otoshi approaches, begin sliding your left foot back and move into a right zenkutsu-dachi. At the same time, hold your left hand about one shoulder-width above your right and reach out with both. (3) Before the oncoming weapon lands, catch it with a hasami nigiri, left hand uppermost. (4) Begin rotating the bo counterclockwise before you. As the staff approaches a horizontal position, move your hands into a jun nigiri, turning your right palm toward the ceiling, your left palm toward the floor. (5-6) Continue the counterclockwise rotation and destroy your adversary's sense of balance. Simultaneously, pull what is now the left section of the staff down toward your left hip. Forcefully crash the other section over and down into the left side of your foe's neck and chin. (7-8) Pivot 90 degrees into a right gyaku-zenkutsu-dachi. Follow-through with your downward thrust, throwing your opponent to the ground and maneuvering the bo out of his control. (9-10) Smoothly pin him there with a strong osae-uke (bar). Use both hands to swing the staff high up on your left side. Then, shoot it down in a strong tsuki-otoshi (reverse downward thrust) to your adversary's eyes.

UNARMED COUNTER TO A YOKO-UCHI (Side Strike)

(1-4) As your opponent's right yoko-uchi approaches, slide your left foot back and move into a right zen-kutsu-dachi. At the same time, reach out with both hands. Before the on-coming weapon lands, catch it with a jun nigiri, right palm toward the ceil-ing. (5-7) Rotating it counterclock-wise slightly, pull the left section of the bo down toward your left hip. Slam the right section over and down into the left side of your opponent's neck or chin. (8-9) Now, dislodge his hold on the shaft by jerking it away from him sharply. (10-11) Then, be-fore he can regain control, counter-attack with a strong tsuki-komi (two-handed thrust) to his mid-section.

138

UNARMED COUNTER TO A MOROTE-ZUKE
(Double-Handed Strike)

(1-3) As your opponent's overhead morote-zuki approaches, slide your left foot back and move into a right zenkutsu-dachi. At the same time, reach upward with both hands. Before the on-coming weapon connects, catch it with a gyaku nigiri. (4-6) Begin a clockwise rotation of the bo. Simultaneously, pivot counterclockwise 180 degrees on your right foot, bringing your left foot out and around into a kiba-dachi. To accommodate this footwork and to force your adversary up behind you, his back against yours, raise the rotating bo high above your head. (7-9) Bend your left knee and lean over it. As you continue the weapon's clockwise rotation, snap the bo past your right shoulder and down before you, flipping your opponent over your right hip and to the ground. (10-11) Now, turn the bo counterclockwise 180 degrees into a horizontal position at your left side, your right hand leading. Simultaneously, slip your right hand into a jun nigiri and slap what is now the forward section of the staff into your opponent's face. (12-13) Use your left hand to slide the staff easily back through your right. Then, stab it forward in a nagashi-zuki (sliding thrust) to his eyes.

BO-JITSU COUNTER TO A RIGHT PUNCH

(1-4) From a left stance, step back with your left foot into a right zen-kutsu-dachi. At the same time, hold the bo with the gyaku nigiri and deflect your opponent's on-coming

punch with a downward morote-uke (double-handed block). (5-6) Then, before he can recover, quickly thrust the staff up in a strong morote-zuki (double-handed thrust) to his throat or chin.

BO-JITSU COUNTER TO A RIGHT FRONT KICK

(1-3) From a left stance, step back with your left foot into a right zenkutsu-dachi. At the same time, hold the bo with the gyaku nigiri and deflect your opponent's on-coming right front kick with a downward morote-uke (double-handed block). (4-5) Then, pull the right section of the staff down toward your rear right. Sharply thrust the left section

forward and up in a gyaku-yoko-uchi
(reverse side strike) to the right side
of your adversary's face. (6-7) Pivot
counterclockwise 90 degrees into a
right gyaku-zenkutsu-dachi. Simultaneously, pull the left section of the
staff down toward your left foot.
Forcefully thrust the right section
forward and up to hit the left side of
your opponent's face.

BO-JITSU COUNTER TO A NANAME-AGE-UCHI
(Diagonal Side Strike)

(1-3) As your opponent's right na-name-age-uchi approaches, step back with your left foot into a right zenkutsu-dachi. At the same time, with your hands in the jun nigiri, right palm toward the ceiling, pull the left section of the staff down toward your rear left. Bring the right section forward, up and in from the outside (that is, the right), using it in a naname-uke (side strike block) to stop the on-coming blow. (4-5) Now, pull the right section of the bo back toward your right shoulder. Shoot

the left section forward and out in a gyaku-gedan-uchi or a gedan-uchi-barai (reverse low strike). Catch the outside of your adversary's right knee forcefully enough to bring him down on it with his back to you. (6-8) Then, angle the bo up over your right shoulder, your right hand to the rear and uppermost. Pull what is now the forward section down toward your left hip. Powerfully thrust the other section forward and down in an uchi-otoshi (overhead strike) to the back of your opponent's neck.

BO-JITSU COUNTER
TO A MOROTE-UKE
(Double-Handed Block)

(1-2) Begin stepping forward with your right foot into a right zenkutsu-dachi. At the same time, hold the bo with the jun nigiri, right palm toward the ceiling. With your left hand leading, raise the weapon over your right shoulder. (3) As you come down into the right zenkutsu-dachi, pull what is now the forward section of the staff down toward your left hip. Attempt to thrust the other end forward and down in an uchi-otoshi (overhead strike). When your opponent counters with an upward morote-uke (double-handed block), (4-5) pull the staff up and back with your right hand. Push it forward and

out with your left. Continue this movement, bringing the bo up through a horizontal position over your right shoulder, your left hand again leading. Thrust what is once again the forward section of the weapon upward, moving through your opponent's chin and between his upraised arms to hit his bo with an uchi-age (upward strike). Use enough force to dislodge his hand(s) and take him out of the morote-uke. (6-8) Before he can regain control, slide your weapon back over your shoulder. Then, shoot it forward in a gyaku-zuki (reverse thrust) to his eyes.

BO-JITSU COUNTER
TO A TSUKI-KOMI
(Two-Handed Thrust)

(1-4) As your opponent's tsuki-komi approaches, pivot toward him into a right zenkutsu-dachi. At the same time, move your hands into a gyaku nigiri. Before the on-coming weapon connects, use the right section of your staff to push it heavily down and to your outside right. (5) Before your adversary can recover, smoothly pull the right section of your bo down to your rear right. Swiftly

thrusting the left section forward and up, hit the right side of his head with a sharp gyaku-yoko-uchi (reverse side strike). (6) Raise the staff over your right shoulder, your left hand leading, both palms toward the floor. (7-8) Then, pull what is now the forward section of the bo down toward your rear left. Forcefully thrust the other section forward and out, finishing off your foe with an uchi-otoshi (overhead strike) to his head.

BO-JITSU COUNTER
TO A MOROTE-ZUKI
(Double-Handed Strike)

(1-4) As your opponent raises his bo for a downward morote-zuki, use the jun nigiri to hold the bo horizontally on your left side, your right palm toward the ceiling and leading. Make sure your feet are in a right stance. Before the attacking weapon connects, swiftly shoot your staff out in a powerful nagashi-zuki (sliding thrust) to your adversary's midsec-

tion. Use enough force to double him over. (5-6) Before he can recover, quickly raise the bo over your right shoulder, your left hand now leading. (7) Then, pull what is now the forward end down toward your right hip. Forcefully thrust the other end forward and down in a strong, finishing uchi-otoshi (overhead strike) to your foe's head.

BO-JITSU COUNTER
TO A YOKO-UCHI
(Side Strike)

(1-3) As your opponent's left yoko-uchi approaches, shift your weight back into a right kokutsu-dachi. Slide your hands into a hasami nigiri, left hand uppermost, and turn the bo into a vertical position before you. Then, firmly bring the staff to your right and stop the on-coming blow with a sideways morote-uke (double-handed block). (4-5) Shift forward into a right zenkutsu-dachi. As you do so, take control of your adversary's weapon. Moving smoothly through the completed morote-uke, push his bo up and to the left with your own. At the same time, use both hands to rotate your staff counterclockwise 180 degrees into a second vertical position before you. (6-7) Maintaining control of your opponent's weapon, continue the counterclockwise rotation. However, pull what is now the lower section of your staff down and back toward your left hip. Push the other section forward, out and down to your low left, simultaneously forcing your opponent's bo down also. (8-10) Before he can react, swiftly snap what is now the forward section of your own staff up into his chin and throat. (11-12) Then, swing it over to your right and down, following-through to throw your adversary to the ground.

KATA

The kata exercise presented here is called *Shushi-No-Kon-Sho* and it includes many of the basics taught in Kihon, Kotei-Kihon and Ido-Kihon. Practicing it diligently gives you a solid and essential understanding of fundamental techniques. In addition, constantly running through this predetermined sequence of executions helps develop smooth, fluid movement, the proper integration of speed and power, rhythm and timing, easy mobility in all directions, nimble manual dexterity and good hand/eye coordination.

While performing this kata and indeed all kata, it is vitally important that you imagine yourself in the actual sparring or fighting situation. To really understand the exercise, give force and purpose to your blocks and strikes. Execute them not merely in and of themselves, but as though they truly deflect attacks and inflict pain. Utilize the concepts of mushin and kime to focus your entire being on each technique, realize its functional meaning in your mind and then carry it out in your actions.

Visualizing yourself in a real situation while performing the kata helps build effective instinctive responses, as in the sparring routines. Again, in order for your instinctive actions to be effective, you must constantly and devotedly practice the exercise, relaxing and paying special attention to your development of mushin and kime.

Remember, too, no matter how proficient you seem to be in bo-jitsu executions, your technique will never be perfect. Perfection is the ever-receding goal toward which you must strive but will never achieve—not even after years of practice. In sparring situations, also, remember that someone more skillful than you always exists. So, work even harder to perfect your own movements.

During your practice sessions, take extra care to prevent injuries either to yourself or to those around you. Bo-jitsu kata are potentially more dangerous than empty-handed forms because they involve a weapon.

SHUSHI-NO-KON-SHO

(1) Assume a musubi-dachi (ready stance). With your right hand, hold the bo vertically behind your right arm and shoulder. Let your left arm hang naturally along your left side. (2-3) Bow at the waist. Then, return to your original upright position. (4) Using your right shoulder as a fulcrum, swing the bo across your body. Angle the lower section toward the outside left. (5) Swing your right arm up in front of your left shoulder and angle the staff up toward the high left. At the same time, reach across with your left hand, catching the bo farther down the shaft with a hasami nigiri (palm hold), palm toward the floor. (6) Bring the bo to a horizontal position at head level by pulling to the right with your right hand, upward and to the left with your left hand. (7) Assume the yoi (ready) position. Keep your right arm straight and bring the bo down vertically in front of your right arm and shoulder. Simultaneously, push it up and to the right with your left hand. End holding your left arm, palm turned away from you, across your face. (8) Detaching your left hand, return it to a position at your left side. (9-10) With your left hand, palm facing forward, again reach up across your face and grasp the bo securely. As you do so, pivot counterclockwise on both feet, turning yourself 45 degrees to the left. (11) Slide your left foot back and assume a solid right zenkutsu-dachi (forward stance). (12) Pushing it forward and down with your left hand, backward and up with your right, bring the bo to a horizontal position over your right shoulder. Slip your right hand around the shaft so your right palm faces the ceiling. (13-14) Pull what is

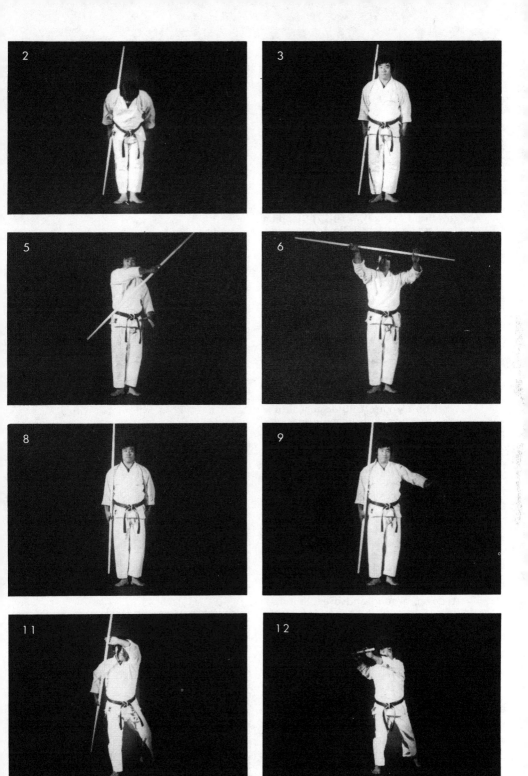

now the forward section of the staff down toward your left hip. Forcefully thrust the other section forward and out in a well-focused uchi-otoshi (overhead strike). (15-17) Stepping forward and to the left with your left foot, move into a shiko-dachi (straddle stance). At the same time, hold the bo on your left side, your right hand leading. Push the staff forward and up. Then, shooting it straight back on a level even with your midsection, deliver a strong tsuki-otoshi (reverse downward thrust) to the rear left. (18-19) Now, thrusting the bo forward again, execute a tsuki-komi (two-handed thrust) to your opponent's stomach. As you do so, keep both feet stationary and straighten your knees. (20-21) Pivoting clockwise, turn yourself 90 degrees into a left gyaku-zenkutsu-dachi (rear defense stance). Simultaneously, use your right hand to pull the bo up and in toward your right shoulder. With your left hand, sweep it down, out and over your left foot. Forcefully thrust what is now the lower section of the weapon out in a gedan-uchi (low strike) to your opponent's shin. (22-24) Now, pivoting counterclockwise 180 degrees, move into a left zenkutsu-dachi. As you turn, rotate the bo clockwise. Use your left hand to pull the bo up over your left shoulder. With your right hand push it down, around and over your left knee. End with the palm of your left hand facing away from you, the palm of your right hand toward the ceiling. Shoot what is now the lower section up in an uchi-age (upward strike) to your opponent's groin. (25-27) Pivoting clockwise on

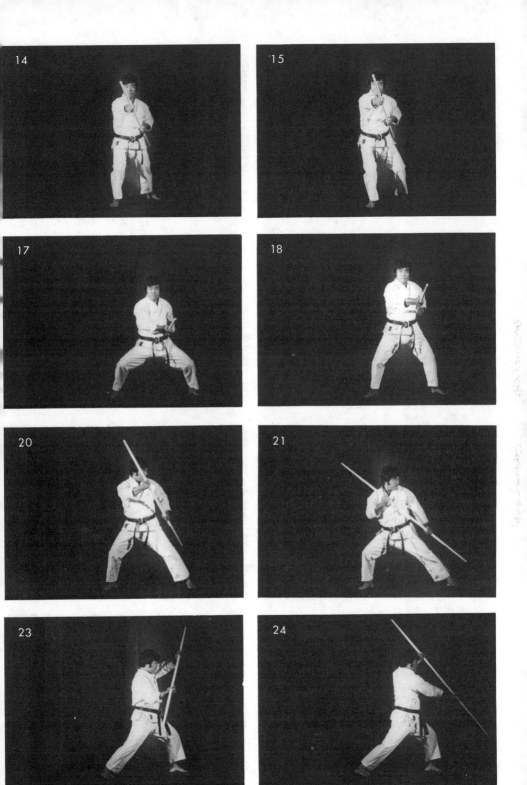

both feet, turn 180 degrees into a right zenkutsu-dachi. At the same time, bring the bo around in a clockwise sweep also. Keep the upper section positioned over your left shoulder, the lower section angled out and down before you. As the staff comes toward your right knee, execute a sideways morote-uke (double-handed block). (28) Now, rotate the bo counterclockwise 180 degrees. Simultaneously, raise it to a horizontal position over your right shoulder, your left hand leading. (29-30) Pull what is now the forward section of the staff down to your left side. Forcefully thrust the other section forward and out in a powerful uchi-otoshi. (31) Begin moving the forward section of the staff to the inside (that is, to your left). (32) Then, pull it upward and (33) back to the outside (that is, to your right) in a firm right yoko-uke (inside to outside block). (34-36) Shift your weight to your left leg and turn yourself counterclockwise 90 degrees. Slide your right foot toward your left, then forward. At the same time, pulling upward and back with your right hand and pushing it downward and out with your left, bring the bo to a horizontal position over your right shoulder, your left hand again leading.

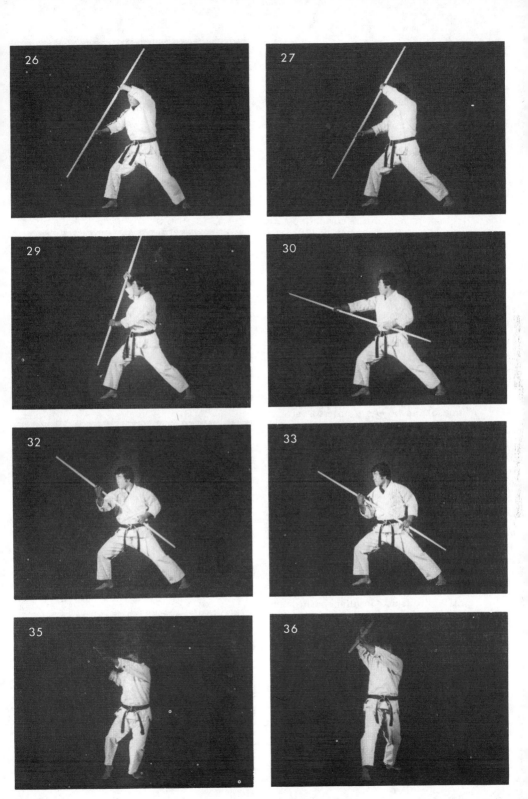

(37-38) Now, as you shift your weight to your right foot and bring your left toward it, jump off both feet. Simultaneously, pull what is now the forward section of the bo down toward your left side and thrust the other section forward and out in a right uchi-otoshi. While completing this technique, keep your back straight, your feet and knees together, to help insure correct posture and smooth movement. (39) Step back with your left foot into a right zenkutsu-dachi. Lower the forward section of the bo and bring it to a horizontal position on your left side, your right hand leading. (40) Begin moving the forward section of the staff to the inside (that is, to your left). (41) Then, pull it upward and back to the outside (that is, to your right) in a strong right yoko-uke (inside to outside block). (42-43) Slide your left foot forward into a heiso-ku-dachi (ready stance). Moving it before you, begin a clockwise rotation of the bo. As it enters a vertical position, your left hand uppermost, assume the yoi (ready) position. Keep your right arm straight and bring the bo down in front of your right arm and shoulder. Hold your left arm, palm facing away from you, across your face. (44-45) Step back with your left foot into a right zenkutsu-dachi. Pushing forward and down with your left hand, backward and up with your right, raise the bo over your right shoulder, your left hand leading. (46-47) Now, as you shift your weight to your right foot and bring your left toward it, jump off both feet. Simultaneously, pull what is now the forward section of the bo down toward your left side and thrust the other section forward and out in a right uchi-otoshi. Again, as you complete this technique, remember to keep your back straight, your feet and knees together. (48) Step back with your left foot into a right zenkutsu-dachi. Lower the forward section of the bo and bring it to a horizontal position on your left side, your right hand leading.

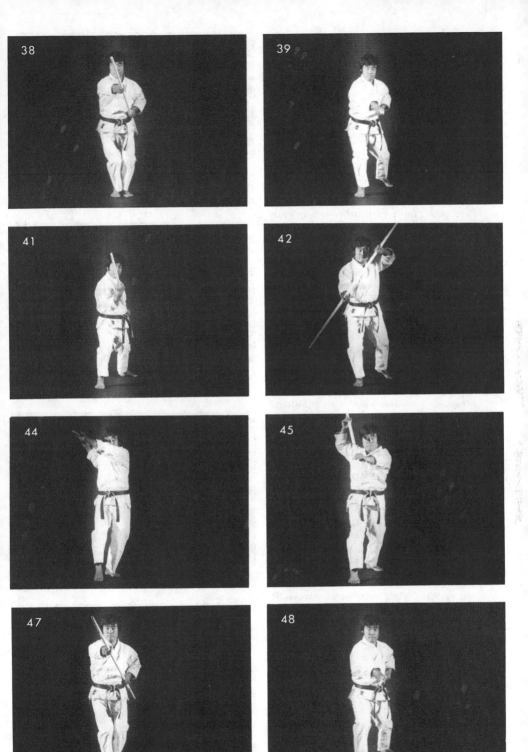

(49) Begin moving the forward section of the staff to the inside (that is, to your left). (50) Then, pull it upward and back to the outside (that is, to your right) in another right yoko-uke. (51-52) Slide your left foot forward into a heisoku dachi. Begin moving the bo before you in a clockwise rotation. As it enters a vertical position, your left hand uppermost, again enter the yoi (ready) position. Keep your right arm straight and bring the bo down in front of your right arm and shoulder. Hold your left arm, palm facing away from you, across your face. (53) Now, slide your right foot forward into a solid right zenkutsu-dachi. Push forward and down with your left hand, backward and up with your right, and raise the bo over your right shoulder, your left hand leading. (54-55) Bring what is now the forward section of the bo down toward your left side and thrust the other section forward and out in a right uchi-otoshi. (56) Lower the forward section of the staff, move it to the inside (that is, to your left), upward and back to the outside (that is, to your right) in another right yoko-uke. (57) With your left foot, step forward and to the left. (58) Turn clockwise into a left gyaku-zenkutsu-dachi. As you do so, use your right hand to pull the bo up and in toward your right shoulder. With your left hand, sweep it down, out over your left foot and (59) into an osae-uke (bar or pinning action) to your opponent's shin. (60) Keeping your left hand stationary, now use your right hand to pull the bo up through it. (61) Then,

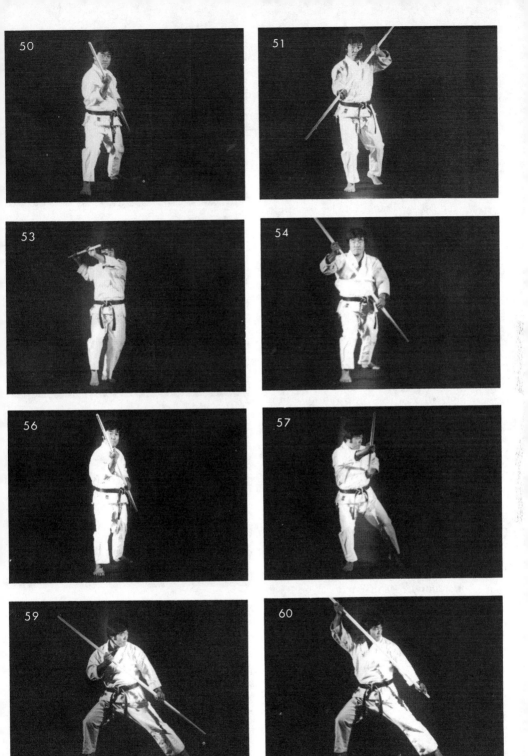

swiftly and smoothly shoot it down and out over your left leg in a tsuki-otoshi (reverse downward thrust) to your opponent's foot. (62-65) Pivoting counterclockwise 180 degrees on your left foot, bring your right foot out and around into a right zenkutsu-dachi. Simultaneously, begin rotating the bo clockwise. As it approaches a vertical position before you, your left hand uppermost, execute a firm tate-uke (vertical block). (66-67) Now, rotating the bo counterclockwise 180 degrees, raise it over your right shoulder, your left hand leading. (68) Pull what is now the forward section of the staff down toward your left side and thrust the other section forward and out in a right uchi-otoshi. (69) Pull up with your right hand, push out with your left and bring the bo to a vertical position before you, your right hand now uppermost. (70) Then, with your right hand, pull the upper section back over your left shoulder. With your left hand, shoot the other section forward, out and up in a gyaku-age-uchi (reverse upward strike) to your opponent's face. (71-72) Pull what is now the forward section of the staff down and back on your left side. Snap the other section forward and out in a short yet effective uchi-otoshi. To insure maximum striking power, be sure your push-pull motion is quick and forceful. (73) With your right hand, lower

what is now the forward section and, (74) in a large circular movement, sweep it back on your outside right. Simultaneously, push the other section forward and up with your left hand. (75) Smoothly move the bo over to your right side and angle it over your right shoulder, your right hand to the rear and uppermost. (76-77) Now, use your left hand to pull the staff down toward your left side. At the same time, use your right hand to arc it forward and out in an uchi-otoshi. (78) Lower the forward section of the weapon. (79) Move it to the inside (that is, to your left) and swing it upward. (80) Then, pull it sharply back to the outside (that is, to your right) in another yoko-uke. (81-83) Turn yourself counter-clockwise into a left gyaku-zenku-tsu-dachi. As you do so, thrust the lower end of your weapon down over your left leg in a snappy osae-uke (bar or pinning action) to your opponent's shin. (84) Keeping your left hand stationary, use your right hand to pull the bo up through it.

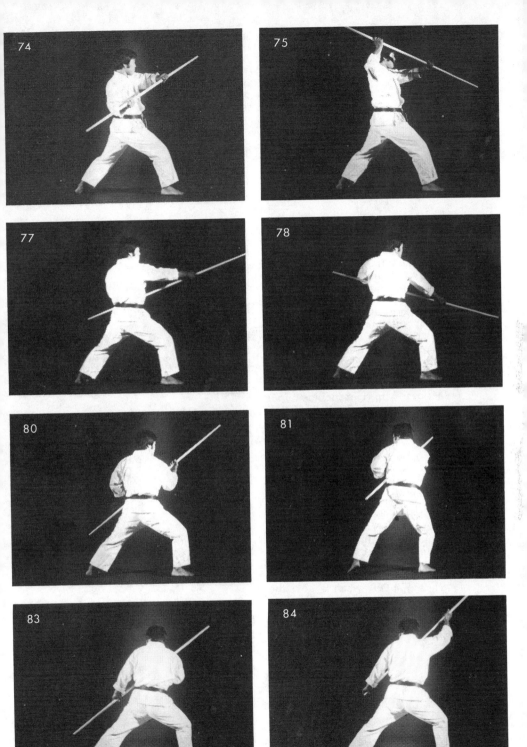

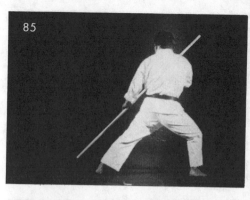

(85) Then, swiftly and smoothly shoot the staff down and out over your left leg in a tsuki-otoshi to your opponent's foot. (86) Bring the bo up slightly out of the tsuki-otoshi. (87-89) Pivoting counterclockwise 180 degrees on your left foot, bring your right foot out and around into a right zenkutsu-dachi. Simultaneously, begin rotating the bo clockwise. As it approaches a vertical position before you, your left hand uppermost, execute a firm tate-uke (vertical block). (90-91) Now, rotating the bo counterclockwise 180 degrees, raise it over your right shoulder, your left hand leading. (92) Pull what is now the forward section of the staff down toward your left side and thrust the other section forward and out in a right uchi-otoshi. (93) Pull up with your right hand, push out with your left and bring the bo to a vertical position before you, your right hand now uppermost. (94-95) Then, with your right hand, pull the upper section back over your left shoulder. With your left hand, shoot the other section forward, out and up in a gyaku-age-uchi (reverse upward strike) to your opponent's face. (96-97) Pull what is now the forward section of the staff down and back on your left side. Snap the

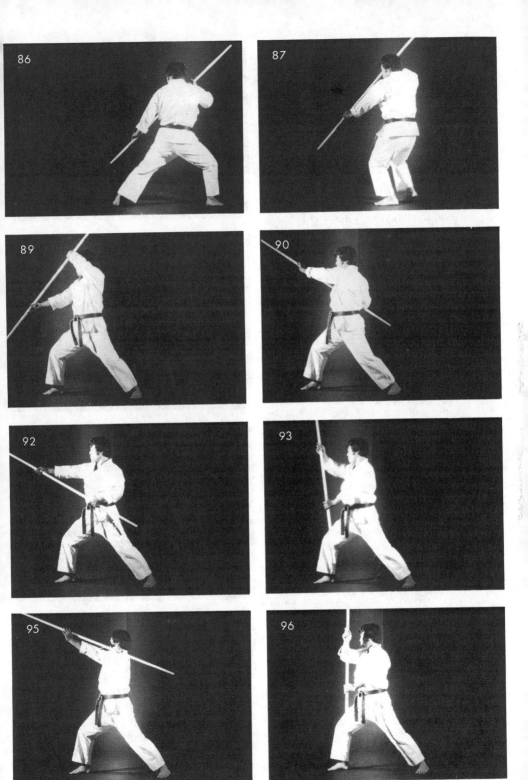

other section forward and out in another short but effective uchi-otoshi. (98) With your right hand, lower what is now the forward section and (99) in a large circular movement, sweep it back on your outside right. Simultaneously, push the other section forward and up with your left hand and move the bo over to your right side. (100) Smoothly angle the weapon over your right shoulder, your right hand to the rear and uppermost. (101) Now, use your left hand to pull the staff down toward your left side. At the same time, use your right hand to arc it forward and out in an uchi-otoshi. (102) Lower the forward section of the staff and move it to the inside (that is, to your left). (103) Then, swing it upward and (104) pull it back sharply to your outside (that is, to your right) in another yoko-uke. (105-106) Bring your left foot toward your right and turn your torso clockwise 90 degrees. Then, pivoting clockwise slightly on your right foot, extend your left in a left gyaku-zenkutsu-dachi. At the same time, use your right hand to pull the bo up in toward your right shoulder. With your left hand, sweep it down, out over your left foot and into an osae-uke to your opponent's shin. (107) Keeping your left hand stationary, now use your right hand to pull the bo up through it. (108) Swiftly and smoothly shoot it down and out over your left leg in a tsuki-otoshi to your opponent's foot.

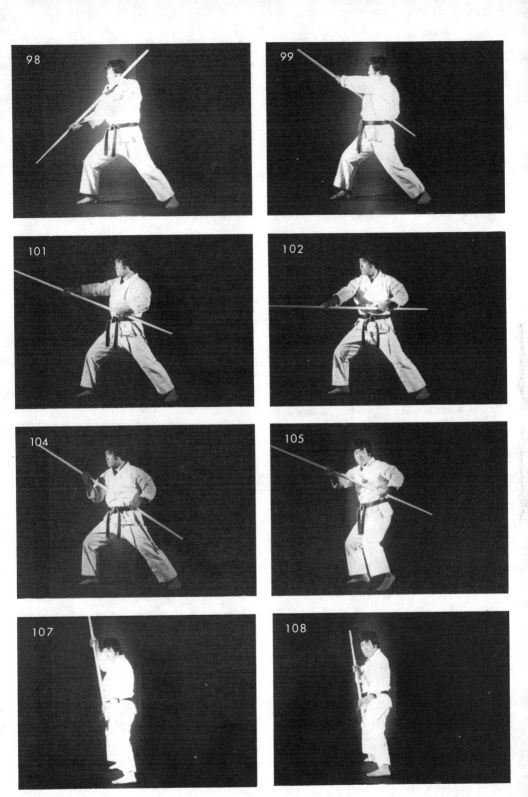

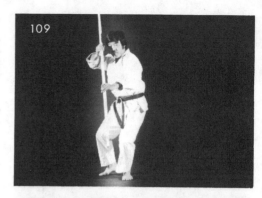

(109-111) Pivoting counterclockwise 180 degrees on your left foot, bring your right foot out and around into a right zenkutsu-dachi. Simultaneously, begin rotating the bo clockwise. As it approaches a vertical position before you, your left hand uppermost, execute a firm tate-uke. (112-113) Now, rotating the bo counterclockwise 180 degrees, raise it over your right shoulder, your left hand leading. (114-115) Pull what is now the forward section of the staff down toward your left side and, with a large arcing motion, thrust the other section forward and out in a right uchi-otoshi. (116) Now, keep your right hand stationary and use your left hand to pull the bo back through it. (117) Then, swiftly and smoothly, shoot the staff forward in a nagashi-zuki (sliding thrust) to your opponent's chin. (118) Lower the forward section of the staff, (119) swing it to your inside (that is, to your left), (120) upward, (121) then back to your outside (that is, to your right) in a firm yoko-uke. (122-123) Turn your torso

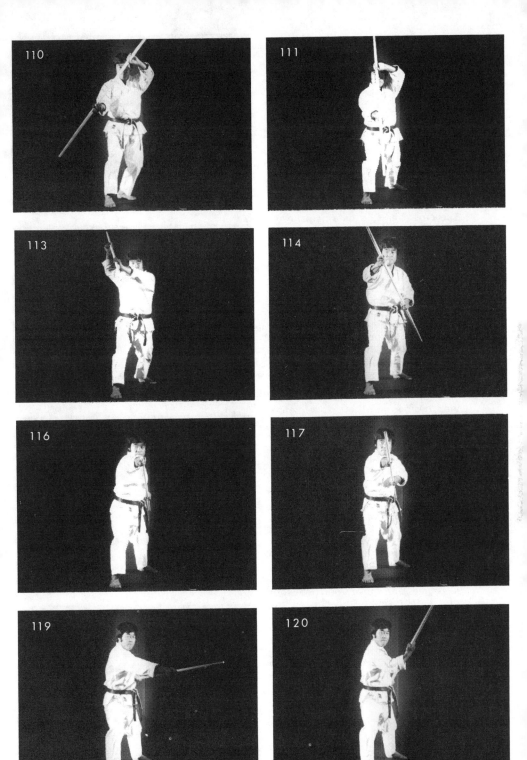

counterclockwise 90 degrees and shift your weight to your left leg. As you do so, move backward by crossing your right foot over your left. The crossover step here helps insure an even, well-coordinated hand execution during the movement to the rear. (124) Step down on your right foot. Position the bo horizontally on your left side, your right hand leading, and sweep the forward section to your inside (that is, to your left). (125) Then, swing it upward and back to your outside (that is, to your right) in a strong yoko-uke. Keep your body low and your step narrow to facilitate proper movement, easy recovery and a smooth entry into your next technique. (126-127) Shift all your weight to your right foot and, raising your left foot before you, swing it up, out and around. At the same time, use both hands to angle the bo over on your right side, your left hand uppermost and leading. (128-129) Keep your right foot in place and stamp down with your left into a kiba-dachi (horse stance). Simultaneously, pull what is now the forward section of the staff back and down on your left side. Snap the other section forward and to your left in a yoko-uchi (side strike) to your opponent's stomach. (130-132) Turn yourself clockwise 90 degrees and move your right foot into a right zenkutsu-dachi. At the same time, begin rotating the bo clockwise before you. As it approaches a vertical position, your left hand uppermost, execute a strong tate-uke. (133) Now, rotating the bo

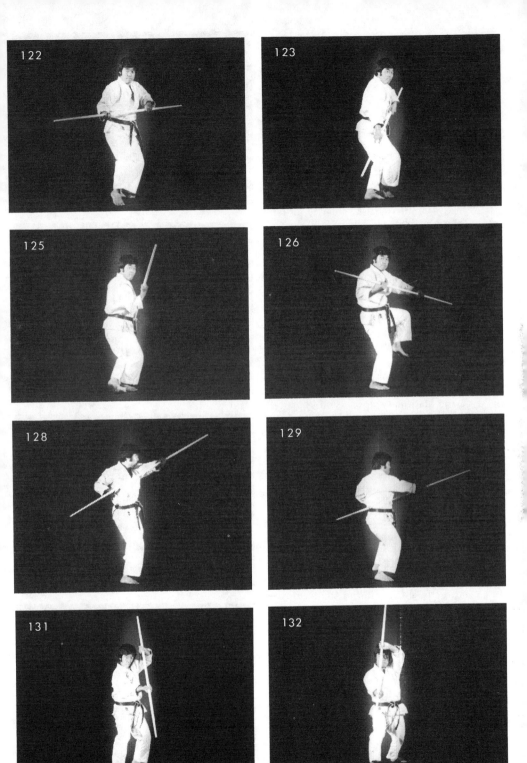

179

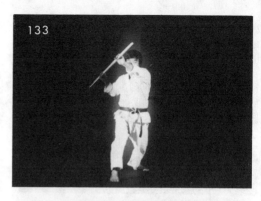

counterclockwise 180 degrees, raise it over your right shoulder, your left hand leading. (134-135) Pull what is now the forward section of the staff down toward your left side and, with a large arcing motion, thrust the other section forward and out in a right uchi-otoshi. (136) Now, keep your right hand stationary and use your left hand to pull the bo easily back through it. (137) Then, swiftly and smoothly pushing with your left hand, shoot the staff forward in a na-gashi-zuki to your opponent's face. Be sure to thrust the bo forward un-til your left hand meets your right. (138-139) Again, keep your right hand stationary and, using your left hand, pull the bo back to its position prior to execution of the sliding thrust. (140) Lower the forward sec-tion of the staff and sweep it to your inside (that is, to your left). (141) Swing it upward, (142) and back to your outside (that is, to your right) in a firm yoko-uke. (143-144) Step back with your right foot into a musubi-dachi (ready stance). Moving it before you, begin a clockwise rotation of the bo. As it enters a vertical position, your left hand uppermost, assume the yoi (ready) position. Keep your right arm straight and bring the bo down in front of your right arm and shoul-der. Hold your left arm, palm facing away from you, across your face.

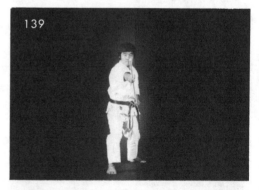

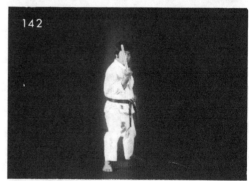

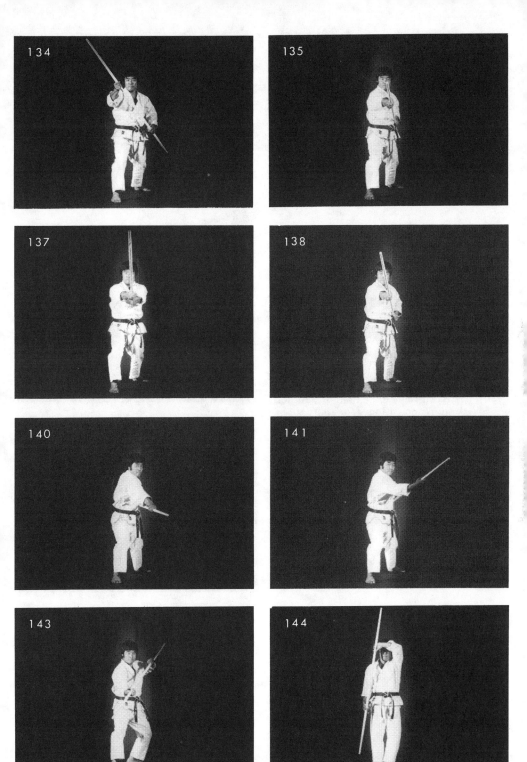

(145-146) Pushing down and to the left with your left hand, pulling up and to the right with your right, rotate the bo counterclockwise 180 degrees. (147) As it approaches a vertical position with your right hand uppermost, release the hold of your left hand. Then, using your right shoulder as a fulcrum, bring the bo down to a vertical position behind your right arm and shoulder. Bring your left arm to your left side and (148) hold both arms along the sides of your body. (149) Bow by bending forward at the waist. (150) Straighten up to return to your original position (as in step no. 1).

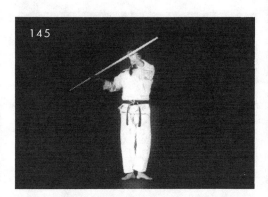

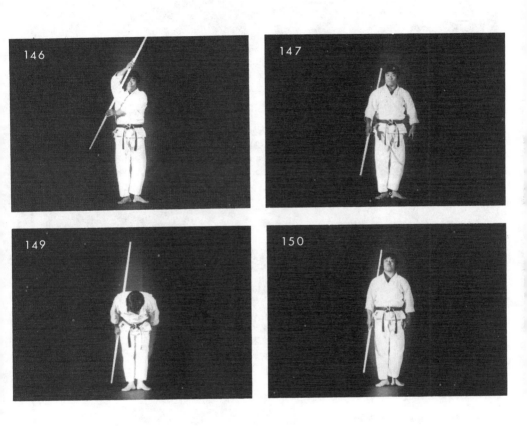